MAN, STATE AND DEITY

Essays in Ancient History

By the same author

The People of Aristophanes
The Greek State
From Solon to Socrates

MAN, STATE AND DEITY

Essays in Ancient History

❦

VICTOR EHRENBERG

METHUEN & CO LTD

First published in 1974
by Methuen & Co Ltd
11 New Fetter Lane, London EC4P 4EE
© *1974 by Victor Ehrenberg*
Printed in Great Britain
by Richard Clay (The Chaucer Press), Ltd
Bungay, Suffolk

ISBN 0 416 79460 2 (hardback)
0 416 79610 9 (paperback)

Distributed in the U.S.A. by
HARPER & ROW PUBLISHERS, INC.
BARNES & NOBLE IMPORT DIVISION

To Lore and Martin Ostwald

Contents

ERRATA

page 40, line 19	for 'Pyrkaeus, the fire-kindler' read 'Pyrphorus, the fire-bearer'
page 121, line 13	for 'praesesi' read 'praeses'
page 122, line 5	for 'princips civium' read 'princeps civium'
page 149, line 7	for 'changes' read 'charges'
page 177, line 5	for 'one' read 'none'
page 191	insert 'Vogt, J., 124'

Acknowledgements

The author and publishers would like to thank the following for permission to reprint material from the sources listed below: Encyclopaedia Britannica International Ltd for 'The Hellenistic Age' from *Encyclopaedia Britannica* (1964); Harvard University Press for 'Caesar's final aims' from *Harvard Studies in Classical Philology*, vol. 68 (1964); Mouton & Co. for 'Freedom – ideal and reality' from *The Living Heritage of Greek Antiquity* (1967); and Verlagshaus Frankfurter Societäts-Druckerei for 'Dike and Eros' from *Frankfurter Zeitung* (4 March 1925).

Preface

This is the last book which I still can hope to produce. It covers a number of essays written (and some of them published) at very different times of my life. I have left them more or less as they were written, though I have inserted a number of corrections and additions, in order to make things clearer. I have also added a few quotations and a few notes (in square brackets), though I have not tried to bring old papers 'up-to-date'. Those papers may be good or bad, strong or weak, but they must stand on their own feet. They cover very different aspects of my scholarly interests, and one of them (Chapter IX) is more in the way of a confession than of scholarship; it is the one which underwent some major changes, especially in its last section. If I have to apologize for all this, I do so, as I do for any repetition or possible contradiction within this collection of essays.

Volumes of this kind, though fairly frequent nowadays, are not favourites with publishers. The more grateful I am to Methuen for their generous attitude and willing help. I have also to thank my friend Professor H. H. Scullard as well as my two sons for reading some parts in typescript and providing useful criticisms.

London, April 1973   V. E.

I

❦

East and West in antiquity[1]

There may have been times when the tremendous importance of the relationship between East and West – in Europe or on the whole earth – was not realized. In the lifetime of the last two or three generations everyone will have felt the impact of the contrasts and conflicts between East and West. I believe it was more or less the same in antiquity, and there will be few people who might prefer a theory recently fashionable: that the invasion of Northern, i.e. Indo-European, intruders into the Mediterranean was of greater impact than continuous relations – friendly or hostile – between East and West.

It is a vast subject, and to press it into one lecture means that much can only be hinted at, and much has to be left out. Moreover, even when restricted to ancient times, it is by no means a clearly defined subject. It can mean mainly the contrast between Europe and Asia, or between the western and the eastern Mediterranean. It will also be more than a question of geography; the contrast of two different spiritual aspects, two ways of the working of the human mind. If we are prepared to see it in its most sweeping (and therefore inaccurate) generalization, we can speak of the god-centred East and the man-centred West.

[1] Translated from an unpublished lecture in German delivered in various forms between 1949 and 1960 at several universities.

I

It goes without saying that those relations and conflicts could be political, economic, social, religious, or of any other sphere of man's life and mind. But we need not try to paint such a multicoloured picture in order to see the whole instead of its parts. There is a clear unity behind the many aspects: history has been shaped by the relations and decisions between East and West to such an extent that behind the various historical forces lies a certain unity, though not uniformity. The facts of history were decisively determined by the moves and happenings between East and West; they were, as it were, the bed of a river which was formed by very different forces. We may have certain concepts of East and West, but they resist all clear definition; that simply does not exist. What I am going to do is to discuss facts of ancient history in the light of the general concept, however nebulous, of the East–West contrast. There can be little doubt that the foundations laid in those centuries are, even if unconsciously, the foundations of all succeeding times.

The history of the ancient world, as seen in its widest aspects, is a unity the centre of which is the Mediterranean. Without denying that a really universal history might be possible, I am speaking of the European history to which Mesopotamia and Egypt belong, to some extent India but not China. History moved from Babylon and the Near East to Greece, and from Greece to Rome, but also directly from Jerusalem to Rome and in the opposite direction from Rome to Constantinople, always East to West or West to East. Very different peoples and civilizations adapted themselves to the new surroundings, essentially because of the climate and rich soil of most of the Mediterranean world. They came from the North like the Persians, Greeks and Italians, or from the South like the Semites to Mesopotamia and Syria; later followed the Celts, Germans, Slavs, Arabs. They all, as far as they became part of the Mediterranean area, shaped its history, accepted the demands of, and were shaped by, their new homes: they 'became Mediterranean'.

The first era of our history took place in the Near East (now usually called the Middle East), in Egypt, Mesopotamia and Asia Minor. Here for the first time in our world, prehistory grew into history. Excavations during the last century or so have revealed the

cultural greatness of these countries, and the evidence is still growing. There are many other important differences, partly determined
by the different race groups, partly by local conditions; but there
are also decisive common features. Just as further east, in the Punjab
and in China, civilizations grew up in the river valleys of Mesopotamia and Egypt where annual flooding brought to the lowlands
the fertile soil which gave these countries their great chance. It was
'the river's gift', as Herodotus calls Egypt, but only because man set
to work on what nature offered him. Dikes and dams and canals
had to be built, even artificial flooding added during the dry sea-
sons. The population grew, and the technical achievement led to
political consolidation and organized administration. Briefly, the
states of the Ancient East were all, though in different ways and in
different mixtures, theocratic, autocratic and bureaucratic: divine
or god-given kings, a caste of priests, a hierarchy of bureaucrats.
May I give you an amusing example of the bureaucratic spirit? An
Egyptian book contains a father's letter to his son, who may have
had a low I.Q. He is advised to do better in order to become a
scribe (an official), not a peasant or a soldier or metal-worker 'who
has fingers like a crocodile' (a suitable comparison if we think of
its thick skin). 'Be a scribe who is free from compulsory work, even
protected against all labour ... When a man works with his hands
he does not dare sleep, for hard labour lies in front of him. No
servant brings him water, no woman bakes bread for him, while his
former school-fellows have become scribes, live according to their
own desires and have servants working for them.' This description sounds, of course, idealized to an almost ironical degree.
Even high officials (they perhaps more than the lower grades) were
dependent, living in fear of the king. But the praise of an official's
comfortable life sounds genuine. Perhaps the highest achievement
of such a bureaucracy, apart from an efficient system of administration, was the use of writing and the creation of a written code of
laws, as it is especially connected with the name of Hammurabi.
It was most important for the development of mankind that these
early autocratic states proclaimed the principle of justice. The laws
of the East, partly by influencing the Greeks and largely by way of
the legislation in the decalogue of the Old Testament, which had

3

a good deal in common with Hammurabi's laws, had, as we all know, a decisive influence on European civilization.

Those empires of the Ancient East with their urban civilization, their peasant serfs, their astonishing achievements in art, architecture, literature, and in particular in science, were above all strong political powers, and the threatening imperialism of Babylon, Assur and Persia was knocking at the doors of the West. Yet the driving force was religion, primitive in many aspects, 'barbarian', full of fear of daemonic powers, reaching a remarkable height in the worship of the sun as the embodiment of truth by the heretic Pharaoh Ikhnaton, and eventually its most spiritual shape in the ethical dualism of Zoroaster and the ethical monotheism of Israel.

When in the second half of the second millennium B.C. the East began to get in nearer touch with the West, they were unequal opposites, the East a vast, consolidated system of states, the heir of high civilizations, the West weak, primitive, still in the era of pre-historic migrations. The only exception was the Minoan civilization of Crete, which had strong connections with Asia Minor and Egypt, but displayed an amazing originality; it belonged neither to the East nor to the West. It was this rich, peaceful and refined civilization which the first Greeks met after they had come from the Balkans and invaded their future home country. The Mycenaean civilization as well as similar centres in Asia Minor, e.g. at Troy, resulted from a mixture of civilizations. Primitive warrior tribes accepted much of that higher Minoan culture, yet without abandoning their own way of life. What emerged was not Greek civilization, though Greeks for a time ruled in Crete, and there was an imported syllabic script (Linear B), used by skilled scribes to put down records in Greek. There also began a tradition of myth and legend which shaped the world of Homer. The Trojan war may have been one of the piratical onslaughts by the Mycenaeans to counter the East beyond the Aegean, even in Syria and Egypt. The warriors who did not settle anywhere outside Greece were followed by colonists. Later, towards the end of the second millennium when new Greek nomads came from the North, a movement culminating in the 'Dorian Migration', there began the Greek colonization of the Aegean and the west coast of Asia Minor, an area that was to be the outpost of the West against the East, and at the same time a fortress and a market. This movement led to what is called the 'Ionian Migration'. The Greeks became heirs to the Eastern world and at the same time its enemies and conquerors, and that is true of the cultural aspects no less than of the military and political ones. Asia Minor, though hellenized only centuries later, had begun on its historical task of being a bridge between East and West.

However, the Greeks had to start again, almost from scratch. After the end of the Minoan and Mycenaean world, long dark centuries followed, the era of Hesiod's Iron Age in the true sense of the word, for it was then that in the Mediterranean the Bronze Age ended. We know very little of the Greeks of the eleventh to ninth centuries. The decisive fact is the emergence of the Greek people and its world of political units, having one language, one religion, one civilization. Politically as well as in its various forms of dialects, cults and cultural developments, it was divided into numberless independent units. The Greeks had closed behind them the gateway from the North through which they had passed themselves, and became Mediterranean. Mixing with earlier Greeks and non-Greeks they were the creators of the first European civilization. It is significant that inside the extending area of Greek settlement the tension between East and West was soon apparent. Furthest to the East, the Ionians and Aeolians were most progressive, living in an urban civilization of prosperity and even luxury, though they had to learn from the 'motherland' the finer crafts, e.g. vase-painting. In general, however, it remains true that the further to the West, the slower were cultural progress and political stabilization.

The world in which the Greeks grew up during the dark centuries had also changed. New powers arose and opened new ways of political expansion. The Phoenicians, a Semitic people, founded cities along the Syrian coast, and their ships sailed the Mediterranean as far as the Pillars of Heracles and beyond. Carthage, founded by Phoenicians in the ninth or eighth century, was the leading Eastern colony in the West. The mysterious people of the Tyrrhenians probably emigrated from the eastern Mediterranean and invaded

Italy, creating the great Etruscan civilization which brought at the same time a great deal of Greek culture to Italy and later – directly and indirectly – to Rome. In the East the cruel military power of Assur advanced to the shores of the Mediterranean and, among other things, forcibly repulsed a landing of Greek colonists in the south of Asia Minor. The relations between East and West grew closer, though hardly less hostile. Symbolic for this process is the creation of the alphabet. Containing earlier imperfect attempts of the East, the Phoenicians created the signs for consonants which the Greeks in the ninth or eighth century accepted and adapted to their own different dialects. Europe owes its most important cultural tool to the East, though it was finally shaped by the creative inventiveness of the Greeks.

About the time when the Phoenician cities began to flourish, the country behind the Phoenician coast, Palestine (or Canaan), was invaded by tribes from the southern desert who became the people of 'Israel', which means 'God fights'. It was a time of war and murder, as it is described at the end of *The Book of Judges*: 'In those days there was no king in Israel: every man did that which was right in his own eyes.' But the external enemy, the Philistines, believed by some scholars to be Indo-Europeans, forced Israel into defence and to a monarchical consolidation. This move was accompanied by religious intensity when the Jewish god Jahve was raised to a position of national monotheism which later opened the way to universal monotheism. The decalogue pronounced clear ethical laws, and gradually over many centuries those books were written, mythological, pious or historical, which all preached the greatness of Israel's god, and not that of its people or its leaders. Thus the religion of Israel was enabled to become the source from which Christianity and Islam originated.

The creation of what we now call the Old Testament is roughly contemporary with the creation of Homer's epics. We shall not deal here with biblical criticism or the Homeric question. The decisive fact is that the two most miraculous literary expressions of the human mind came into the world at about the same time, and could not be more different. On the Eastern side the miracle of divine revelation was predominant, on the Western were the deeds of heroic men. Yet there were also heroic men under the guidance of God, and on the other side is the myth, however anthropomorphic, of the Olympians. From the stories and images of Homer and the Old Testament sprang two never-ending rivers which fertilized the history of the European mind and largely prevented it from becoming a dry desert. The Bible and Homer (often called the Bible of the Greeks) are opposites, bearing witness to the Eastern and the Western minds. However, even in this contrast is something they have in common. Man, whether created by God or a godlike hero, has to face the task of shaping his own fate and put into harmony his own will and the laws of divine world order. Here we touch on the deepest foundations of Europe. We shall have to speak of both sides, but first of the Greeks.

Greek literature started with its greatest revelation, and Homer remained the lasting companion of most Greeks from schooldays to the grave. In the great epics are reflected not only prehistory, myth and fairytale but also a completely new vision of world order. Instead of the Eastern view that the world is created and ruled by external divine forces, for the Greek the world itself is full of gods. Πάντα πλήρη θεῶν. It is in this world that man lives and in himself combines the great general rule, the unity of freedom and order. Apart from a few passing movements, Greek religion never fettered mind or reason, and that is why the Greeks were the first philosophers, the first who tried to understand both the *kosmos* and their own minds. Greek philosophy and science learned from discoveries and researches of the East, but they alone recognized the true principle of it all, rational definition. The word philosophy, the 'love for wisdom', speaks for itself, expressing the heroic fight of the European mind for that truth which the East received in divine revelation, that heroic and tragic fight which all the time led to the mountain tops and again into the depths of the abyss, but did not forget the final goal: to try to understand the macrocosm of the world and the microcosm of the human mind.

This, of course, does not mean that all Greeks were philosophers. It is always dangerous to speak of *the* Greeks. We know what most of them thought of those thinkers who, as with other peoples, were generally regarded as useless dreamers. There always was (and is)

7

a gap between the beliefs of the masses and the theories of the intellectuals. Philosophy was only one of the ways to human perfection. Most Greeks were well aware of the dangers of human greatness; but though they might condemn *hubris*, they knew nothing of the humility of the East. We might say that the Greeks saw the legitimate end of human endeavours in the satanic word of the serpent: '*eritis sicut Deus scientes bonum et malum*'.

The autonomy of man was achieved within the framework of the state. By the founding of Greek colonies, the Greek form of state, the polis, was brought to all the shores of the Mediterranean and even the Black Sea. Land-hungry peasants, impoverished townsfolk, traders, adventurers, they all went out to sail largely unknown seas; to settle in unknown lands; and to found new autonomous Greek city-states. Thus, the kind of state which for the first time in human history represented a community of free citizens became the basis of Western civilization. That remains true even though the society of the polis could only exist with the help of slavery. The West found in Aristotle's 'political animal', the citizen bound to the polis, the counterpart to Eastern politics which were in the hands of the king or the god whom he served. The people, apart from the king's officials, knew nothing of politics, and the only form of patriotism was religious nationalism. In the polis everything was political, even religion, and it is political freedom, though rarely fully accomplished, that Greek culture was built upon. There is no need to idealize reality. With all its faults and insufficiencies, the Greek state was an expression of the will of the people and the foundation of culture. It faced its crucial test in the victories over Persia and Carthage, and experienced its highest flowering in the Periclean Age. It also influenced the East. The Greek features of the Persian court in Aeschylus' *Persae* do not prove that either way, but the famous coin of Tissaphernes with his own head on the front, and the Athenian owl on its back, does.

The Periclean Age saw at the same time the first signs of the break-up of the polis community. The autonomous state gradually disintegrated because of the increasing autonomy of the individual. The Sophists and Socrates marked the beginning of the end for the old Greek civilization, though it still took a long time till the end came. Socrates had tried to combine the new principle of individual responsibility with the traditional idea of citizenship. His death sealed the fate of his attempt but, more than through all his teaching and questioning, it was his martyrdom that made him for all time the great witness of truth.

The fourth century prepared the Greeks for their new oecumenical task, although the two great philosophers of that century, Plato and Aristotle, as far as their political philosophy went, looked backwards and did not understand the signs of the time. It was Alexander who by his conquests and his empire, not least by the latter's break-up, created a new world to which both East and West belonged. Now the Greeks were the main support of a civilization which we call Hellenistic, but which owed a great deal to the East, especially in public administration and economic organization. A feature prevalent in most of the Hellenistic monarchies, also the result of both Eastern and Western influences, was the cult of the deified ruler. Meeting and mixing of East and West occurred everywhere and in all ways of life. Indian art created the picture of a Greek-looking Buddha, and at least one book of the Bible, *Ecclesiastes*, is full of Greek wisdom and Greek scepticism; the mysteries of Eastern gods, on the other hand, with their ecstatic rites, entered the life of Greek cities, and educated Greeks began to study Babylonian astrology. There are many other examples of the mating between East and West, some of them rather absurd. May I quote from the correspondence between one of the purely Indian, but hellenized, Mauryan kings and one of the Seleucids? The Indian asked for three items and was prepared to pay for them: a certain sweet drink, dried figs from Asia Minor and a Greek sophist. The answer was: 'I shall send you the figs and the wine, but a sophist, according to Greek views, is not an article of sale' (*Fr. Hist. Gr.* IV, 421). There were, however, Greek sophists and artists who went as far as India, and though the rule of Greek kings in Bactria and India did not last long, we still hear of a Greek ruler in India about 30 B.C. who was a vassal of the emperor of China. Thus, even the Far East was connected with the West, and not only by the traders who along the famous Silk Road crossed the whole width of Asia.

The Hellenistic dynasties were all Alexander's successors, but they inherited only parts of his empire. The Antigonids were kings of the Macedonians, leaders of a free people and heads of the Greek federation of states. The Ptolemies ruled the state of the Pharaohs, inheriting its organization and its wealth; but they also accepted Alexandria as their capital as well as the trade centre of the Mediterranean, which Alexander had created. The Seleucids were kings of Asia, heirs to the Persian empire and founders of Greek colonies deep into the East. The Pergamene kings ruled over Asia Minor. They were all Macedonians, but heirs to Greek culture, and they felt themselves the masters of the barbarians of the East. Only the Greek kings in Bactria and India, as we have been taught by the late Dr Tarn, tried to follow Alexander's final idea of fusing Eastern and Western peoples into a new unit.

The world was hellenized, and the Greeks, although citizens of their poleis, grew oecumenical. It was a hellenized Phoenician who founded a new philosophical school at Athens, its teaching based on the idea of the unity of mankind: Zeno, the founder of the Stoa. He talked of the *kosmopolis*, that is to say, the Greek polis grew into the idea of a world state. That remained an Utopian idea, but the citizen of that state which never became reality, the citizen of the world, became a new spiritual figure. On the other hand, the new gospel of rational ethics, as preached by the Stoics, found a home especially in Rome and strongly influenced the future masters of the world.

In fact, the Hellenistic Age was not much closer to the ideal of the brotherhood of mankind than earlier periods. There was no end of wars and of social crises, and slavery grew in extent. The cosmopolitan philosopher remained a lonely figure. The poor and oppressed found little hope in the doctrines of philosophy. They tried to find irrational and emotional support, they were looking for beliefs and miracles. That was partly the heritage of their own folklore, but it also brought the religions of the East to the West. Eastern and Western deities grew together in 'syncretic' figures, though the full impact of this movement did not become real before it found its place in the political unity of the Roman empire.

For some time past, military and political power and also its moral force had emanated from the new centre of Rome. The give and take between the Greeks and the East lost its importance to the tension between the western and the eastern Mediterranean. A man was a Greek then not by his descent but by his culture; Zeno is an example for many others. But a Roman at that time was only the man who belonged to the new imperial people of the West.

The Romans, by their conquest of Italy and their victories over Carthage, had become the masters, but also the cultural representatives of the West. They learnt a great deal from the Greeks, but they had enough character of their own to create a new civilization, which was the first of all secondhand civilizations. In a sense the Romans, depending as they did on the Greeks in literature, art, philosophy and to some extent even in religion, were the first humanists of history. Roman politics were at an early stage purely nationalist and imperialist, but in spite of self-interest, corruption and brutality, they served the interest of mankind. Much was bad and cruel; but Rome's self-interest grew into the interest of the world, and it was Rome that gave to the world peace, law and order, and prosperity. As far as this can be ascribed to an individual it was Augustus whose deliberately Roman policy put a halt to the expansion of the Hellenistic East when he defeated Antony and Cleopatra. Nobody is a more obvious witness to the spirit of that age of the *Pax Romana* than Virgil. The Italian who wrote the *Georgics* was also the poet of the *Aeneid*, which was a national Roman epic, but great enough to become a poem for humanity. In the Fourth *Eclogue*, written as early as 40 B.C., the historical moment, the hoped-for end of the civil wars, is seen as part of a divine plan for humanity and a prophecy which made Virgil an *anima naturaliter Christiana*. He preached the great leading ideas which were to dominate the work of Augustus and the better of his successors. For about two centuries, unity and peace were preserved within the *Orbis Romanus*. It was not a young creative epoch, but it was not without greatness, and its achievements in fostering peace and prosperity were stupendous. It is quite wrong to deprive that period of all value of its own, as Spengler and Toynbee have done. Success was due less to the work of individual good rulers such as Tiberius and Claudius or Trajan and Marcus Aurelius (or, in fact, impeded by the misrule of other emperors) than to the fact that in a system, well organized on the whole, millions of people were living and working in peace and contentment in all parts of the empire.

There is, on the other hand, no doubt that, despite great stability, there was a general development by which the well-tempered political, social and intellectual life changed its character. Largely under the influence of the East, the Augustan principate gradually became the despotism of mad emperors or military upstarts, and eventually the autocratic rule of the *Dominus et Deus*, the deified emperor. Roman citizenship, and that implied possible positions in administration and army, was increasingly granted to provincial non-Romans, even to barbarians who had entered the empire from beyond its frontiers. It was actually the most highly educated of all emperors, Marcus Aurelius, who settled barbarian tribes as frontier guards within the borders of the empire, and the *Constitutio Antonina* of 212 made every free man within the empire a Roman citizen. Italy had lost its pre-eminence. Moreover, modern archaeological research, inscriptions and papyri have taught us many things of which the literary sources knew nothing. Thus it may be appropriate to say a little more about a small provincial town just *because* it was small and unimportant and therefore in many ways must have been typical.

Doura-Europus, in recent decades excavated by the Americans, was founded by the Seleucids about 300 B.C., but the double name is proof of an earlier settlement. The Greek town, as many others, was planned according to the scheme of rectangular crossing streets, which had been popular ever since Hippodamus invented it in the fifth century B.C. Administration and official language in Doura-Europus for a long time were Greek, but the population was mixed. Situated on the banks of the Euphrates, it was under strong Eastern influence, and the town flourished under Parthian rule until the Romans arrived in the second century A.D. and put a fortified military camp next to the town. But its character did not yet change. A number of Eastern gods had their cults there, some under their original names, others hellenized. It was not a rich town, but its citizens were prosperous and ambitious enough to build fine houses and temples. Amazing frescoes have been discovered which display a mixture of Hellenistic art (similar to those we see in Pompeii) and a strong influence of purely Oriental elements. As with the Parthians this is a mixed civilization, but the Hellenistic part remained rather superficial. We notice a hieratic stiffness, a lack of realism, no individual life; but a fine decorative style.

About the middle of the third century A.D., Doura-Europus was destroyed by the Sassanids. Shortly before, two buildings had been erected, a church and a synagogue. Both were small, and their congregations can only have been small; but they were wealthy, and both buildings were richly decorated with frescoes. Those of the synagogue are particularly impressive: scenes of biblical history with images of men, Moses prominently among them, and also the hand of God reaching out from the clouds of heaven. Above the sacred niche is even a painting of Orpheus among the animals, probably a symbol of the spread of true religion among the Gentiles. All that, however, is in complete contrast to the Jewish tradition, going back to the second commandment, not to make 'any graven image, or any likeness' of anything in heaven or on earth. Obviously this Jewish community was strongly influenced by foreign culture, whether Greek or Iranian or both. The church is less unique: it is part of that early Christian art which depicts Jesus as a Greek youth, an Apollo rather than the Lord of Christianity. It was later in the East, in Byzantium, that the hieratic picture was created which culminated in the magnificent abstract portrait of the Pantokrator, Christ the ruler of the world.

But I am anticipating. I only wished to show how in a small outpost of the Roman empire, religions and civilizations met and mixed. And yet East and West, even at that time, were still distinct and largely separate. In the West, a Latin culture of its own had taken root, while the East, in spite of Roman officials, soldiers and merchants, saved or regained its specific character. One of the great features of the Roman empire is the absence of artificial uniformity, of *Gleichschaltung*. The dualism of East and West existed and was to become the chief problem for the rulers of the empire.

The so-called good emperors of the second century A.D., from Trajan to Marcus, had ruled with both vigour and justice. It was a happy period, according to Gibbon the happiest in human history. Its leading idea was *humanitas*, the Roman form of educated

13

humanity, which would be congenial to an eighteenth-century historian, but rather alien – too alien in fact – to the nineteenth and twentieth centuries. Still, even that happy period of the second century had its troubles and dangers, and a century later the destructive forces had grown so strong that the empire went through its severest crisis – the beginning of the end.

It is impossible for me to describe the decline and fall of the empire in any detail. Historians have been trying to find many causes of the decline, but no single one was decisive, though all had their share in it: enemies from outside the empire, inner decomposition, the rule by soldiers, the disappearance of whole groups of the population, bureaucratic corruption, spiritual enervation, lack of technical knowledge and – we have to talk about that – the growth of Christianity. In all this the tensions between East and West were often predominant.

Before and after A.D. 300, three great autocrats who were all born in the middle of the empire, in Illyria (as it were, between East and West), tried to stop the decline and disruption. Aurelian wanted to make Rome once again a strong centre. However, to do so he built a powerful wall around the city; it is still there, but it meant that Rome had to be defended at her own gates, and no longer at the frontiers of the empire. Diocletian divided imperial power among two Augusti and two Caesares, an artificial scheme of partial responsibility that broke down soon after his own abdication, but made a return to a unified rule almost impossible. Diocletian did not think of a divided empire, but for the first time several capitals existed, and Rome was no longer one of them. Administrative reorganization, on the other hand, served the coherence of the empire. Constantine, though he established his own autocracy, founded the Rome of the East, his own city, Constantinople. It was to be the capital of the whole empire, but at the same time a stronghold against the new enemies from the East and the North-east, an ever-increasing threat. In Constantine's realm little was left of the Roman state, still less of Greek freedom. Everything turned Eastern – the emperor, the administration, the social organization. The steady advance of the East was assured, nowhere more clearly than in its most creative sphere, in religion.

Ever since the stabilization of Roman rule, the Roman forms of religious worship had spread everywhere, above all the cults of the *Dea Roma* and of the emperors, dead or alive. This official religion was an expression of the unity of the empire, a political rather than a religious matter. There was no question of belief or even emotional feeling, apart from the expected loyalty towards Rome and the emperor. Yet it was possible for Greeks in Asia Minor to celebrate Augustus's birthday by words such as these (*OGI* 458): 'Providence which rules our life has given perfection to this life by the birth of Augustus who was created full of virtue for the sake of mankind. To us and to those after us, he came as the saviour who brought peace and good order to the world . . . The day of his divine birth started for the world the good tidings (εὐαγγελία) of his work.' This sounds like the language of true faith, and yet was hardly more than an expression of official servility. Emperor worship knew of no believing congregation, but it is significant for the spirit of the time that such a public decree could be shaped in the language of faith. Hope and faith evoked the picture of redemption, of deliverance by divine powers. Even among the educated, rational philosophy had lost much ground; the ideals of the polis citizen or of the sage belonged to the past. Once the gates were opened Eastern religion inundated the West. It arrived in the most diverse forms, from the most awesome to simply ridiculous superstition. Two things were lost in the processes: the belief in the autonomy of the human mind and, on the other hand, atheism and agnosticism.

We cannot describe, not even in its outlines, the picture of the religious world in the first centuries A.D.[2] It would be a painting of many colours, of greatest variety, in which Christianity would be only one of many Eastern religions. Most of them tried to make proselytes everywhere, and some were serious rivals in establishing an oecumenical church. Above all there was a general trend towards monotheism which met the teachings of philosophy and astrology.

Yet Christianity, even seen from a purely historical point of view without any emphasis on divine interference, was different. It was

[2] [Generally, cf. A. D. Nock *Cambridge Anc. Hist.* X (1934), 465 ff; XII (1939), 409 ff.; also G. E. M. de Ste Croix *Didaskalos* IV (1972), 61 ff.]

different first because it was an offspring of Judaism, of its unique monotheism and the ethics of the prophets. Moreover, it combined with the Jewish legacy that of pagan antiquity: Greek philosophy, chiefly Neo-Platonism, and Roman law and policy were decisive in shaping Christian theology and the Christian church respectively. Christianity was also unique in its swift expansion. That was to a great extent due to the many communities of the Jewish Diaspora; it was for the hellenized Jews of Alexandria that in the third and second centuries B.C. the Greek translation of the Bible, the *Septuagint*, was made which had the strongest influence on the Christian church. On the other hand, when Titus destroyed the temple in Jerusalem, the spiritual centre of Judaism, many Jews turned Christian and propagated the new creed to the pagans. Christianity met also the full resistance of the secular powers, and the Christian martyrs were one of the strongest bonds in the growth of the early church. Last but not least, Christianity was unique because of the person of Jesus and the efforts of St Paul. What seized the fervour and the imagination was that God had become Man, a reversal of the widespread belief that men could be divine. Christianity bridged the Eastern separation between God and Man, but still more definitely destroyed the man-centred concept of the West. The God of justice and the Platonic Eros were replaced by God's love for Man and Man's for God, by *Agape*.

For the swift expansion of Christianity was also decisive in that it grew up within the frontiers of the unity of the Roman empire, a fact which for the first time became manifest and important when St Paul said to the Roman governor (*Acts* 25, 10) 'I stand at Caesar's judgement seat, where I ought to be judged... I appeal unto Caesar,' and the governor replied: 'Unto Caesar shalt thou go.'

Without discussing the fascinating struggles within the Christian church and giving more than a few hints of the complicated story of the early centuries A.D., we can explain, at least to some extent, the miracle which we may define as the greatest event in our history. Obviously the new religion fitted into the tensions between East and West to both of which it belonged, but was soon broken up into Greek and Latin Christianity. The union of state and church, both supposed to be universal, as accomplished by Constantine, produced the secular power of the church, but bound it to the fate of the state. When Western Rome perished, the Western church under the bishop of Rome was its heir, while state and church were one in the Caesaropapism of Byzantium. The young peoples from the North created new political forms and ideas in the West, but accepted Christianity and with it the reverence for the eternal name of Rome. They became part of the declining empire of the West and agreed to the spiritual rule of the Pope. From the East, Justinian once more tried to restore the unity of the whole empire, and the Christian emperor, rather surprisingly, could be greeted once more as *deus terrenus*, as god on earth. But Eastern Rome had its own enormous tasks, above all the defence of the Mediterranean and Europe against Sassanids and Arabs in the South as well as Slavs and Huns in the North. Byzantium was a most important power as well as the guardian of a great civilization. From there, the Slavs were Christianized and received a legacy, if much watered-down, of Classical antiquity. It is often forgotten that for many centuries Byzantium protected and saved Europe and Western civilization.

Another rarely recognized task of Byzantium was the preservation of pre-Papal Christianity. All attempts at re-union miscarried, and if the Eastern church for a long time became sterile, it still today shows some features of early Christianity. Above all, it never – or hardly ever – was a secular power. If in the later Middle Ages Byzantium was culturally influenced by the West, it is of course well known that it preserved the ancient heritage, till the West was able to accept and to recreate it. For many centuries the monks of the East had read and copied the books of Greek literature, till after 1453 they brought them to Italy on their flight from the Turks.

In the West, the ancient world had ceased to exist for almost a thousand years. It has often been taken as a symbolic fact that in the same year 529 Justinian closed the university of Athens (and it is one of history's jokes that the teachers of this first and last Greek university found refuge at the Persian court), and St Benedictus founded the first monastery of the West on Monte Cassino. The end of antiquity coincided with the beginning of the Middle Ages. A century later the rapid ascent of the Islam started. The peoples of history were now Celts, Germans, Slavs and Arabs, and for a time the relations between North and South were more important than those between East and West. Even so, the latter remained alive and often dangerous, though no longer restricted to the Mediterranean.

Here it is time to stop. Between the events I have tried to discuss and today were many centuries in which the world changed more than once. It would be superficial and senseless to draw close parallels between the past and the present. But in a deeper sense history still teaches. There are two opposite answers to the question of what the relations between East and West really mean. One is the famous saying of Kipling, who knew his India:

> East is East and West is West,
> And never the twain shall meet.

But we have seen that the contrasts and conflicts between East and West again and again led to new and fertile effects. Thus we better remember, even in the justified fears and dangers of our own time, Goethe's words:

> Gottes ist der Orient,
> Gottes ist der Okzident,
> Nord- und südliches Gelände
> Ruht im Schutze seiner Hände.

2

Freedom – ideal and reality[1]

When I was invited to present this lecture – and in German – I had quite a variety of objections. It seemed to me more fitting to speak about freedom in English than in German. But that was not an essential consideration. What was really essential was the vast scope of the subject, which seemed more suitable for a political philosopher than for a mere historian. In addition, there was the almost unbelievable task of speaking about freedom in the city of Pericles. When I accepted the invitation I was fully aware that I was inadequately equipped for the task (and this is not false modesty), but I hoped to be able to say something that would lead away from the common catchphrases. I can offer little more than a few suggestions for discussion, and nobody, I think, will expect to hear anything final.

'Freedom' is one of the great ideals, perhaps the greatest, that have inspired mankind – 'La Liberté' as Delacroix painted it on the barricades, 'die Freiheit' for which Beethoven wrote Fidelio. It was the Greeks who invented the word and the ideal. The word, except in modern Greek ('elefteria'), has been lost, and replaced by the

[1] Lecture delivered in German at the Congress of the *Fédération européenne de la Culture* at Athens, 1964, within the general theme of 'The Living Heritage of Greek Antiquity', and later published under this title (Mouton 1967).

Germanic 'freithum' or 'friheit' or the Roman 'libertas'. In English
there are even two words for it: freedom and liberty. They mean
the same, but differ slightly. Indeed, freedom and freedom are not
always the same, and many who use the word are by no means
clear about its essential meaning. More often than not they talk at
cross-purposes.

The freedom of which I want to speak today is in essence –
positive or negative – political liberty. I therefore exclude *a limine*
concepts such as Roosevelt's 'Four Freedoms', though in a sense I
include them. 'Freedom from Want' and 'Freedom from Fear' are
of the utmost importance to the majority of mankind who suffer
poverty and anxiety, and 'Freedom from Hunger' has become the
rallying slogan of a worldwide campaign of charity, but none of
them have much to do with actual political liberty. Here, however, I
must raise an objection to my own argument, for it can rightly be
said that without an economic minimum all talk of liberty is an
illusion. It has not yet been decided which system is best suited to
create that economic guarantee without destroying liberty. It has
been said that the slave could enjoy freedom from want, and the
prisoner behind bars (at least in general) is free from fear. Even
Solon's proud claim that he had liberated Mother Earth which had
hitherto been enslaved (by the mortgage stones that were everywhere to be found), even that was just a metaphor and related only
indirectly to human liberty. The Greeks have taught us what liberty
could be, and that it is not a gift of nature but something to be
fought for. It was an ideal, and as such indivisible. In modern times,
however, a distinction has been made between several concepts of
liberty, and this is useful, even though no full agreement has been
reached. We can speak of three different yet associated types of
liberty. First, there is the liberty of the state (national freedom), the
freedom of a community from alien domination or despotism.
Secondly, there is the political liberty of the citizen within the state.
And thirdly, there is personal liberty, the independence of the
individual. The latter includes, for example, the artist's freedom
of expression, which is perhaps the purest form of this kind of
liberty.

The first, then, is the liberty of the state. 'Sons of the Hellenes' went up the cry before the battle of Salamis in Aeschylus' *Persians*, 'Arise! Fight for the freedom of your fatherland, for the freedom of your wives and children, for the seats of the gods and the graves of your ancestors – everything is at stake!' Even before Salamis, after the first sea battle off Artemisium, Pindar sang that there 'the sons of the Athenians erected the shining pedestal of liberty'. To the king of the Macedonians, who offered to mediate after Salamis, the Athenians replied, according to Herodotus (8,143): 'We know we are weaker than the Persians, but our freedom is so dear to us that we shall defend ourselves with all our might, and not negotiate.' For Herodotus, the war with the Persians was not a national war (at that time there was no such thing), but a fight for freedom against despotism, at the same time external liberty of the state, and political freedom from despotic rule. You can see how different forms of freedom unite and become one.

For the liberty and independence of the state the Greeks had another word: *autonomia*, the freedom of the state to live in accordance with its own laws, τοῖς ἑαυτῶν νόμοις χρῆσθαι. The combination of *eleutheria* and *autonomia*, which we so often find in the inscriptions of state treaties, played a dominant part in the national consciousness of the Greeks of the fifth and fourth centuries. It embodied the independence of every individual 'polis'. Yet by the same token it revealed the perils that threatened the whole political world of the Greeks.

Athens was the champion of freedom because it also understood freedom most strongly in the sense of civic liberty. Sparta – we need only think of Thermopylae – fought no less for the freedom of the Greek states. But all too soon both states sinned against the freedom of the others. They had entered into alliances, and their allies became increasingly dependent upon them. In retrospect the struggle for freedom seemed indeed to have served rather the ends of imperialism. Athens could speak openly of its subjects, and Pericles like Cleon called the Attic empire a tyranny. Liberty for one's own state meant at the same time the will to dominate others. In the fratricidal Peloponnesian war, the Spartans could claim they were bringing freedom and autonomy to the other Greeks. In his speech to the citizens of Acanthus on the Chalcidice peninsula, the

Spartan Brasidas made the situation quite clear. Acanthus was a member of the Athenian empire. Freedom meant revolt and peril, but Brasidas wisely told them that they could be just as unfree under the rule of the many as of the few. However, if they refused his terms, he threatened town and country with destruction. They chose a dubious freedom, a gift pressed upon them by persuasion and force. Time and again the individual city-state's will to dominate strengthened or broke the resistance of the others. State autonomy meant a splitting-up, a division that ruled out all possibility of unifying all Greek states, even of establishing common peace between them (*koine eirene*). The idea of political unity never even occurred to the Greeks, and it was not until they came under Macedonian rule that they found the way at least to peace among the various states.

Political discord, imperialistic power politics, and later a withdrawal from all politics – these were some of the consequences of that kind of liberty. And yet throughout the centuries the ideal of the liberty of the state has never lost its power. The Greeks' struggle for liberation from Turkish rule, with which the history of modern Hellas begins, was consciously under the impact of the deeds and events of 490 and 480 B.C. Lord Byron, who passionately espoused the Grecian cause and gave his life for it, cried:

> Yet, Freedom! yet thy banner, torn but flying,
> Streams like the thunderstorm against the wind.

Freedom of the state meant battling against the wind, against oppositions and powers that seemed overwhelming. What constantly prompted this struggle for freedom was the desire, even of small nations, for self-government, for autonomy. In the language of diplomacy since 1918 it became the small nations' right of self-determination. It was this that broke up the Hapsburg empire, it is this that lives again in the explosive aspirations of the so-called developing countries. Here are great opportunities and great dangers, dangers for the individual state and for the society of states as a whole. May be, freedom among the nations is just a dream, and in the last resort perhaps not even a good one. But history is not concerned with that. History shows time and again that a people would rather have self-government, with all its difficulties and uncertainties, than live under foreign rule no matter how well-meaning.

The Greeks have demonstrated for us that the autonomy of states can lead to chaos and to new enslavement. Nationalism is a child of freedom, but it can happen that the child kills its mother. In the stresses and strains between disunity and foreign rule the Greeks nevertheless gave birth to a new, fruitful idea, which was at least partly successful: that idea was the association of states on a federal basis. In the fourth and third centuries there were confederations or leagues and federal states, which as political powers were a better match than the polis for the territorial monarchies. Internally they preserved the freedom of the city-state. It is noteworthy that the principle of popular representation, the representative system, found its first practical expression here, inasmuch as each member of the federation sent an elected delegate to the federal council or assembly. It will be difficult to establish a direct connection with the modern parliamentary system, but political freedom had already then, as in the democracy of today, become an indirect participation in government. This indeed brings us again to the second form of freedom, the political liberty of the individual with a right to vote, the freedom of the enfranchised citizen. Wherever we turn we find that the Greeks tried out for themselves what later had to be started afresh and carried out by reform and revolution.

As regards the freedom of the individual, we are first confronted with the disturbing impression that, notwithstanding the contradiction of certain thinkers (to whom, however, neither Plato nor Aristotle belonged) the Greeks did not know of 'human rights' (the 'rights of man'), and regarded slavery as natural and inevitable. Greek slaves in general did not fare badly, but they were and remained slaves; only very few were ever set free, and that did not mean complete freedom socially. In Marxist doctrine the Greeks are branded once and for all as a 'society of slave-owners'. But this view disregards three fundamental facts. In the first place it is wrong to assume that the Greek economy was based entirely or even predominantly on slavery. Secondly, it should not be forgotten that there had never before been a society without slaves, and the Greeks at any rate were the first to question the principle of slavery. Finally, it is a sad truth that right up to the present day there have been, and there still are, slaves, even though they go by different names. If poverty coupled with political or economic dependence, whether tied or not to a place or a particular group of people, and the absence of security from acts of despotism and arbitrary imprisonment, if all this makes a slave, then there have been slaves at all times, even though not simply for sale on the market. I wonder whether there is any symbolic significance in the fact that '*doulewo*' in modern Greek means simply 'to work'. The Greek, still less the Roman, slave enjoyed little legal protection, and torture and flogging were all too often a matter of course. It is not our intention to make excuses for the institution of slavery in antiquity, but it should at least be understood in its historical context, and not blindly condemned.

Slavery had also the effect of making the free man much more keenly aware of his freedom. In Greek literature there are innumerable references to the fate of the slaves, especially the female ones, which is pityingly contrasted with freedom. Yet the Greeks were far from feeling what might be called a sense of obligation when you are free, as it is expressed in Abraham Lincoln's words: 'In giving freedom to the slave, we assure freedom to the free.' Freedom as non-slavery was a negative concept, charged with strong emotional undertones, but even as a mere ideal hardly understandable. The way to freedom led through the different kinds of freedom. From one kind, others can be won. Or, as Kant better expressed it: 'One cannot mature to freedom unless one has previously been set free.' Freedom pure and simple, the condition distinguishing the free man from the slave, is an illusion, but one that has moved mountains. 'Freedom,' says Schiller, 'belongs only to the realm of dreams.' He was thinking of the terrors of the French Revolution, when liberty and equality of all men became dependent on fraternity, and from that we are today farther removed than the later Greeks or the Roman Stoic on the throne, whose dream it was.

The struggle for freedom was mainly concerned with the freedom of the individual. And the question is: freedom from what and to what end? Contemporary theorists distinguish between political and individual freedom; I would prefer to call them freedom *within* the state and freedom *from* the state. They cannot always be kept clearly distinct from each other, and we shall see that opinions on freedom in ancient Greek democracy (let alone in the modern one) can be in complete contrast. Only one thing is certain: individual freedom is in the last resort possible only within the freedom of the state or national freedom, though that does not provide a guarantee.

Freedom within the state is something the Greeks experienced and can teach us, also the problems it raises. The polis was the community of its citizens; freedom was always the freedom of the community, expressed most clearly of course in democracy. But it was the Spartan Demaratus who said to the king of the Persians (Hdt. 7, 104): 'The Spartans are free, but not in all things free; for above them as their master is the law.' It was 'King Nomos' who governed the city-state. The freedom of its citizens was subject to the rule of law, and varied according to the nature of the laws. John Locke stated: 'The object of laws is not to abolish or restrict liberty, but to preserve and strengthen it.' In other words, they should govern the community, but only as the servants of the community as a whole. Legality and the rule of law are not identical; Hitler made that only too evident. Laws can be acts of despotism. However people understood it, the maxim still applies: *salus populi suprema lex*. Likewise, to quote Cicero: '*omnes legum servi sumus ut liberi esse possumus.*' The nature of the laws in Sparta undoubtedly left little room for any real political freedom of the citizen. If the quoted words on *nomos* show that the Greeks were aware that political freedom is only possible under the law, it is simply a confirmation of the other non-Greek component of Western political thought – the Ten Commandments of Mount Sinai. At the same time, however, it becomes clear that the distinction between political and individual liberty is not self-evident, but fraught with all the problems inherent in the very concept of freedom.

This is shown by the completely different ways in which Greek freedom has been interpreted in the nineteenth and twentieth centuries. The father of modern liberalism, Benjamin Constant, had chiefly the image of Sparta in his mind when, in a famous speech, he described the Greek state as an organization of coercion.

Athens he regarded to some extent as the exception to the rule. For him Greek liberty was the collective participation of the citizens in the state, which implied the suppression of the individual. These views determined the approach of many later historians. Fustel de Coulanges, in his 'Cité Antique', took the Greek polis and ancient Rome as a practically omnipotent church, and spoke of the '*empire absolu qu'elle exerçait sur ses membres*'. Jacob Burckhardt refers to the 'merciless City-State'. George Grote, on the other hand, praised his beloved Athens as the home of individual liberty, and this belief was shared by German Classicism from Schiller, Hölderlin and Humboldt to Ernst Curtius. Even Hegel, remarkably enough, stated that the liberty of the individual was to be found in Greece. According to him, only in Rome individual liberty was strictly suppressed. Later Gustave Glotz, who for French scholarship overruled the great Fustel de Coulanges, wrote that in Athens '*la liberté individuelle est absolue*'. To find our way out of this maze of conflicting opinions, we had best turn again to the Greeks themselves. The lines of communication with the present day will appear as we go along.

Sources are most abundant for Athens, and no state claimed more than Athens to be the nursery of freedom. At the beginning of the sixth century, Solon finally abolished the debts which put the poor peasant into serfdom. He also granted every Athenian citizen the right to take legal action on behalf of any other citizen believed to have been wronged. Therewith, the conditions were created for the political liberty of the individual citizen, a kind of *habeas corpus* charter on which Athenian liberty was founded. The Athenians themselves regarded the tyrannicide of Harmodius and Aristogeiton as the act that gave them liberty. This belief was based on the popular definition of liberty as the refusal of being ruled by one individual. The tyrannicide was a legend and, like so many legends, unhistorical. It was the harmless Hipparchus they slew, while his brother, the actual ruler Hippias, continued to rule for several years after, even with a much harder hand than before. Nevertheless, the tyrannicide had become a symbol, just as the storming of the Bastille symbolized the overthrow of the ancient régime. The actual liberation of Athens from tyranny came through Spartan intervention and through the work of the second great legislator of Athens, Cleisthenes the Alcmaeonid.

But at this point the ideas tend to become confused. For what Cleisthenes created was democracy, which he called *isonomia*; the same word is used in the drinking song celebrating the tyrannicides, and Herodotus calls it 'the fairest of all names'. It means 'equal distribution of rights', a principle from which Athenian democracy in the next two centuries was to draw the full consequences. It is interesting to note that the word appears in English in the seventeenth century as 'isonomy' and, echoing Herodotus, was described as 'the most agreeable and specious title'. Later it was superseded by the terms 'rule of law' or 'equality of law'. Thus Cleisthenes had an almost direct influence on the moulding of political ideas in modern libertarian England.

Freedom and democracy were closely related concepts, but not identical; they both display many and various shades of meaning. The vital point is that in democracy the idea of equality went side by side with the idea of freedom, and often enough took its place; what mattered was collective freedom as the will of the majority. It has at all times been difficult to strike a proper balance between the so-called will of the people and the rights of the individual. Equality before the law can in reality mean inequality and injustice. Men are not born equal, nor are they equal before the law. I recall the bitter comment of Anatole France: '*La majestueuse égalité des lois, qui interdit au riche comme au pauvre de coucher sous les ponts, de mendier dans les rues, et de voler du pain.*' Like every other constitution, democracy has to be constantly regained. Even within the framework of the world of Greek states with their similar constitutions, Athens committed a serious political blunder in attempting to impose her own system on others. Let this be a lesson to the present time. A form of government, a political structure, that has grown and has its roots in the democracies of the Western world cannot be simply transplanted in uncultivated ground or in ground where the conditions of growth are dissimilar.

When we speak of Athenian democracy it is natural to quote the document which at all times has been regarded as the culmination of all democratic literature. I refer, of course, to the Funeral Speech

(Epitaphios) which Thucydides puts into the mouth of Pericles. We need not deal with the conventional parts even in this particular oration, nor with its undue idealization. As Plato hinted in *Menexenos*, we must beware of taking everything in this speech too literally, that is as a pure reflection of reality. There remains enough of profound truth.

Pericles (or should we say Thucydides?) believed in his ideas, that is to say he saw in them more than an ideal. Of Athenian democracy he said: 'In personal matters all citizens are equal before the law.' Personal achievement, not wealth, is decisive for a citizen's political activity. 'We conduct our political lives as free men; in our private lives we are free of suspicion, and leave everyone to act as he pleases.' Thus, the claim is asserted that the life of the individual is free: but, Pericles continues, '*dia deos*, through fear, we obey the laws, above all the unwritten laws that bring shame upon those who do wrong to others'. Fear is used here in the sense not of being afraid but of standing in awe, rather in the way we speak of the fear of God. It is the greatness of the Periclean ideal that freedom under the law also permits, indeed seems to guarantee, the free development of personality. Pericles said (and the words are famous): 'We are lovers of beauty without extravagance, and of wisdom without unmanliness.' These negative qualities are expressions of personal freedom. Is the claim in accordance with reality? There is no simple yes or no, but it applies in many cases. What is more difficult is to follow the speaker in accepting the free obedience of the citizen as a general and accepted norm. The harmony demanded between freedom and subordination remained, on account of the imperfection of human nature, a Utopian ideal. Quite soon, and notably in the case of Plato himself, began that decisive reaction against political reality that drove leading aristocrats into foreign service, and many citizens into mercenary armies, leaving at home in the end an apolitical bourgeoisie. But we know that once there existed the unconditional unity of liberty and obedience, of the individual and the law. We recall the end of Plato's *Crito*, where the laws themselves speak to Socrates, condemned to death. Socrates persuades Crito that it is more important to obey the laws even than to save one's life. This is the sublime example of a heroic sacrifice for the state, when Socrates lays down his life, fully aware that he has suffered injustice, but convinced that the verdict of the people's tribunal is supreme and that no individual has the right to weaken the authority of the law. The laws tell Socrates that he has suffered wrong at the hands of men, but that one wrong does not undo another. We are confronted with the most tragic instance of how freedom must ultimately be wrecked by reality. *Summum ius summa iniuria.*

Is it therefore true that, as Benjamin Constant asserts, freedom in antiquity consisted merely in '*le partage du pouvoir social entre tous les citoyens*'? Did the total of citizens exercise coercive powers? I do not think we can adopt a categorical 'either-or' approach to this question. One thing, however, is certain: collective liberty was infinitely stronger than individual liberty. Undoubtedly influential was the fact that the city-state was a society united in common cult. The part played by the 'hubris' concept in Greek thought shows their awareness of the overbearing pride that men are prone to, and hence the excessive freedom the individual may claim for himself. Nevertheless, any comparison of the city-state with a church is misleading, and the age of Pericles, in which the idea of liberty culminated, was simultaneously a time of religious doubt and growing rationalism. Yet even if – as I certainly believe – there was no absolute individual freedom in Greek antiquity, does that imply there was none at all? Does, for instance, the law attributed to Solon that no citizen was allowed to remain neutral in domestic strife, mean there was no real political freedom? We know of many examples to the contrary. Above all, for many years there had not been any direct taxes, as they were regarded as a restriction of civic liberty. Prosperous citizens therefore made voluntary money contributions, such as towards the equipment of a trireme, or the performance of a tragedy. Non-political people – Pericles' useless *apragmones* – were at least left alone. Thus, there was in fifth century Athens Timon, the very prototype of the misanthropic individualist. Theoretical and influential opponents of democracy like Plato were allowed to live and teach freely at Athens. Socrates himself, during his trial, believing that the law convicted him unjustly, appealed to his judges, that is to the sovereign people, to change the law. This is undoubtedly political individual liberty of the highest order. But even that was liberty under the law. The Greeks never knew absolute freedom; indeed, it has never existed, for it would lead to anarchy and to the dissolution of any social order. Freedom and order are inseparable, and order in the words of Ortega y Gasset is 'not external pressure brought to bear upon society, but the equilibrium treated within society'.

The will of the majority that governs every democracy is admittedly a good safeguard of liberty, but by no means an absolute one. The trial by potsherds (*ostrakismos*), which allowed the people of Athens to banish a citizen for ten years, was an inadequate instrument easily abused. When we read the names of Aristeides, Themistocles, Cimon, etc., scratched on ancient potsherds, often wrongly spelt, we may be excused from casting some doubt on the propriety of popular sovereignty. In its decline Athenian democracy demonstrated that the resolutions of the masses cannot only be mistaken, they can also be tyrannical. It can be said in general that democratic revolutions, deposing a tyrant, led only too often to new tyranny. When the Athenian people had the right to govern, they only proved their inability to do so. When the people's assembly complained that it was not allowed to take decisions as it wished, it shows the same threat to freedom that comes from the contrary demand of the individual to live as he wants to live, without consideration for the community.

Liberty in Classical Athens was, of course, 'responsible liberty', but it included some of those freedoms which, although not absolute, belong to the absolute imperatives of modern liberalism. Freedom of conscience was, it is true, not one of them. Broadminded though Greek religion was, it was nevertheless possible for politics to exploit the device of impeachment for impiety, as proved by the trials of the friends of Pericles and of Socrates himself. It was possible because the state was at the same time a community with common cults. On the other hand, one only needs to read Aristophanes to see the extent to which the Greek could make fun of both men *and* gods. Let us not forget that Homer himself told jocular and scandalous anecdotes about the gods. Athenian liberty was first and foremost *parrhesia*, freedom of speech, which presupposes freedom of thought and guarantees freedom of discussion, the essential right of democratic existence. It even went so far that Aristophanes, for example, displayed defeatism in denouncing the war being waged at the time. That is the direct precedent of our freedom of the press, and there also was, even under Pericles, an attempt made (and very quickly abandoned) to introduce censorship of comedy. There was freedom of movement – no passports, no customs control, apart from the collectors of harbour duties. What did not exist was an express, legal recognition of the individual; presumably it was unnecessary.

There remains the great question as to how far freedom and democracy go together. The fact that there can be no true freedom in an authoritarian state was proved by Sparta and is confirmed by modern instances. Even that democracy which means the absolute rule of party bureaucracy or ideology is a denial of freedom, and at best replaces it by the promotion of previously underprivileged sections of society.

What can be said about the system we call democracy in the Western world? We all know that in this system, too, freedom has its limits, not only in the obvious rule of law but also in the weaknesses of the system and of human beings. It is not my task to describe in detail the nature of ancient Greek or modern democracy, but some comments on the principles seem to be called for. The essential thing is the coexistence of two ideals – freedom and equality – which is in the last resort unattainable and incompatible. Is there any such thing as equality of freedom? Whereas in a democracy it is the will of the majority that reigns supreme (or should do), the idea of freedom – and hence the liberalism of Constant via Mill to Hayek – demands that the individual, and naturally every minority, should have the possibility of standing up against the will of the majority. Whereas freedom in a democracy consists in the direct or indirect participation of all citizens in government, the individual invokes the rights of man and considers that the existence of the state is only justifiable – more or less – in so far as it protects the fundamental rights of the individual. This was the line taken by Wilhelm von Humboldt in his 'Ideas on an attempt to determine the limits of activity of the State'. This brings us near the image of the 'Night-watchman-State', whose sole task is to look after the security of its citizens in internal and external relations. Modern democracy, however, is essentially no longer liberal but social. The modern state is meant to provide for education, nourishment and health of its citizens – the ideal is the welfare state. We live in an age in which, not least because of the overwhelming demands of natural science and technology, the omnipotence of the state, even though clad in the trappings of democracy, seems to be fully established. It is therefore all the more important that the freedom of the individual should preserve that proud power to hurl for the sake of truth, against the state and its all too human representatives, its thundering 'J'accuse'.

The idea that the state only existed to protect its citizens was completely foreign to the Greeks. It probably goes back no farther than to Rousseau, even though the church accepted St Paul's words (I *Cor.* 9:19) 'Though I be free from all men, I have made myself servant unto all . . .', words on which Luther could base his tract 'On the Liberty of a Christian'. The idea, however, that the Reformation brought liberty is wrong. Even free will itself quit the field in favour of divine grace, and how could religious freedom exist when '*cuius regio, eius religio*' became the ruling principle? Montesquieu had a decisive influence on the modern development though he had learnt more from Rome than from Hellas. He believed that the political freedom of the citizen was secure in the constitutional state, and he took as his model contemporary England, that same England which, in the eighteenth century, had a corrupt parliament and a pitiable monarchy. I cannot of course deal with the whole development in any detail, but the idea of natural law as the basis of human freedom played an important part. At first a higher law than that of men, a divine law, was recognized by the people of Israel and the Greeks in the law of God or the gods. Then the Greeks (and only the Greeks) secularized it and set it against tradition, and hence against religion: Nature against Convention, Physis against Nomos. Thus, they created the conditions for a development which, although in widely diverse forms, led from the Sophists via Aristotle to the European Middle Ages, and then to Grotius, Hobbes and Rousseau. With the American and French Revolutions and the revolutions of the nineteenth century, the rights of man became the slogan of progress – and notwithstanding its problematic nature, anything but an empty slogan.

The liberty preached by the French Revolution was felt to be in direct succession to the liberty of antiquity, but the development of the constitutional state, created in opposition to absolutism to become the modern parliamentarian system, is, in spite of certain Greek antecedents, to be an independent and original creation. Parliamentary democracy is no ideal; nevertheless, its critics should not forget that it tolerates far fewer unjustifiable privileges than any other form of government.

Freedom as a natural right takes us finally to inner freedom. The Sophist Antiphon preached: 'The commandments of law are essentially arbitrary, those of nature spring from necessity.' He draws from this the immoral conclusion that one should obey the laws of the state in public, but one's own nature in private. 'What the laws declare as useful puts nature in chains; what nature dictates is freedom.' Greeks, Jews and Christians, on the other hand, recognized the moral value of inner freedom, right down to Kant's categorical imperative. Montaigne says: '*Potentissimus est qui se habet in potestate*' (He is strongest who has himself under control). This 'power over oneself' has often led to a turning away from the world. But it is this alone that can make men fully responsible to themselves and to their fellow men. The latest version, if I understand it rightly, is the existentialist idea of being 'condemned to freedom', the creative freedom in the face of nothingness, when freedom is in peril to be the 'baseless basis of values'. Against this nihilism I must emphasize that inner freedom is the ultimate consequence of the fact that freedom is a truly moral value, whereas the reality of life is by no means purely moral. This proves, however, that one should not forget political freedom for the sake of inner freedom.

Once again we return to the ancient Greeks. I cannot find with them that absolute realization of individual freedom that many have postulated. But I do see, not merely the ideal of the absolute liberty of the state, which the Greeks sealed with their blood, but also fundamental sections of freedom in political life. True, the city-state continuously restricted the circle of its fully enfranchised citizens, not least in democracy, but it gave its citizens full political liberty, though limiting their individual freedom. Freedom within the state was a general fact, freedom *from* the state was the exception. All this was possible because the Greek city-state was a small state in a narrow area, with no more than a few thousand citizens. It was thus able to form a human society whose members were bound to the whole, not by compulsion but by nature; this implies, however, that personal liberty was fundamentally political. When we try to understand the nature of the Greek state, as it really was, without applying Roman or modern ideas, the mist surrounding the Greek concept of freedom lifts, and we at last understand that, though it was different from the concept of freedom in the nineteenth and twentieth centuries, it was nevertheless its ancestor.

3

Prometheus[1]

Prometheus is a curiously vague personality in Greek myth. He is one of the less important gods. We know of only one cult of importance, at Athens, where he was the god of potters, worshipped sometimes with Hephaestus (the blacksmith) and Athena, who was also the patron of metal workers. Here Prometheus had one annual festival when there was a torchlight race. It seems that he had as a sort of title '*pyrphorus*', i.e. fire-bearer. The fire and the craftsmanship of the potter (very important at Athens) based on the use of fire are closely connected with Prometheus and his cult.

In literature we have the evidence of two major poets dealing with him at considerable length, Hesiod and Aeschylus (*c.* 700 and 525–456). Otherwise there are only incidental passages, some of which had a great influence on later writers like Goethe and Shelley. The story, for example, that Prometheus formed men and, especially, women from clay is first mentioned in *New Comedy* (late fourth century B.C.), but may be much older. In Plato's *Protagoras*, he appears as a benefactor of mankind, though with limited powers. What was he originally?

We must assume that there is a story behind his name. The name is an artefact, a symbol, not the name of a god or a Titan but the

[1] Unpublished lecture delivered as part of Professor Glatzer's course on Job at Brandeis University in 1962.

title of a being of supreme intelligence, foreseeing the future. We do not know how it was first used, but we can say it was the result of a rationalizing myth. When we meet Prometheus in literature, the previous story is forgotten for ever. We have to deal with Prometheus in Hesiod and in Aeschylus.

Hesiod is the only epic poet in the succession of Homer we can still read – apart, of course, from much later writers. He was very different from Homer, a didactic poet who in one poem, 'Works and Days', deals with a litigation against his brother for the family farm, and at the same time presents a vivid picture of a poor farmer's life in Boeotia. In his other poem, 'Theogony', he traces the origins of the gods from Chaos in the beginning to Zeus and his fellow gods and their offspring. This is mainly a series of genealogies, often contradictory, but is none the less a serious attempt, very important to the Greeks, to bring order into mythology. It is clear that there were always good and evil forces in the world. To some extent this is also the contrast between Zeus and his father Kronos, or between the present gods and the Titans or Giants of the former generation. Their fight is one of the most favoured themes of Greek myth and art. But it is also significant that among the Titans were, for example, Themis, guardian of sacred order, and Mnemosyne, Memory, mother of the Muses. Prometheus too belongs to the older generation, son of Iapetus, an otherwise unknown figure (perhaps to do with the Semitic Japhet?). Prometheus' brothers were Atlas, holding the earth on his shoulders; Menoetius, one of those whom Zeus threw into Tartarus; and Epimetheus, whose name, in some stories, was formed in contrast to that of Prometheus.

Prometheus' story appears in both of Hesiod's poems, but with slight differences. The important thing is that Prometheus is a cunning, clever person who tries to cheat Zeus. But from the start Prometheus is the friend of mankind, punished as men are punished, by cruel torture (the feeding of the eagle) 'because he matched himself in wisdom against Zeus'. A second reason is that Prometheus has stolen the fire which Zeus wishes to keep away from men and which was a symbol for practical knowledge. In response, Zeus sends Pandora, a beautiful girl to whom every god has given something to make her more seductive. Epimetheus (and this may be the

story to explain his name) receives her, despite the warnings of
Prometheus against any presents from Zeus. She has a jar, and by
opening its lid she frees all evils, diseases, etc., putting the lid back
only to keep in Hope, the only power of help to men among their
toils and evils. The worst of all evils is woman. Misogyny was widespread among Greek writers. Hesiod describes women as 'no
helpers in hateful poverty, but only in wealth' (though this attitude
of his is not quite consistent). Prometheus himself is not really a
heroic figure, and his friendship for man brings the worst evils to
him as well as to them. Zeus is all-powerful and all-knowing, but
not a good god. Nor is he evil. Power and justice are somehow
mixed up in him, but not really united. This is partly so because
Hesiod uses earlier crude myths as well as his own more civilized
views. He believes in a just Zeus, 'who gives prosperity to the man
who knows righteousness and is willing to speak it'. Dike (Justice)
is Zeus' favourite daughter. At the same time, he is the victorious
ruler in his fighting strength and full power.

From a fragment of Hesiod we also learn that Prometheus married
Pronoia; her name is equivalent to his. Their children were Deu-
calion and Pyrrha, the only survivors of the great flood, and their
son was Hellen, ancestor of the Greeks. Thus, Prometheus became
the Noah of Greek mythology.

According to Hesiod the world is full of good and evil things.
On the whole he is a pessimist. Men lived free from toil and evil
before Pandora opened her jar. The myth of the five ages, ever
declining from one to the next through human sins and faults and
the will of Zeus, is very similar. Even the present Iron Age will
disappear one day, and then the last good things – love, shame,
justice, reverence – will have gone.

It was Aeschylus who changed Hesiod's picture of Prometheus
and gave him the greatness and heroic stature which influenced all
later versions. The extant drama *Prometheus Bound* is a great, even
a terrifying tragedy. Its deeper meaning is much disputed and
difficult to understand, but the chief thing is the suffering god contrasted with an all-powerful, tyrannical, cruel Zeus. We have only
this one complete play, most likely the first of a trilogy, which
makes understanding even more difficult.

Prometheus is here the son of Gaia, the Earth goddess, who is identical with Themis ('one form of many names'). She is an ancient oracle deity and Prometheus learns from her the future. No father is mentioned, and no brother Epimetheus; in fact he could hardly be a son of Themis, who was also a goddess of wisdom and the good order of the world.

The scene is set in the wild mountains of Scythia. Prometheus is being chained to the rock by order of Zeus. Hephaestus is the unwilling instrument; he is urged on by Zeus' creatures Kratos and Bia, Power and Force. Prometheus is being punished because he stole the fire. Kratos says: 'For that he must give the gods their due, that he may learn to love Zeus' tyranny, and cease the championship of man.' Prometheus had actually helped to conquer the Giants and to establish Zeus' rule. But Themis told him about a prophecy that Zeus, by a certain union and the birth of a son stronger than his father, would destroy his own reign (Thetis – Achilles). Prometheus refuses to disclose the secret of that union, and his punishment is increased. He has seen the divine rulers (Uranos and Kronos) overthrown, and he hopes for the downfall of the third, Zeus. This, we may say now, would be contrary to Aeschylus' own views as expressed in all his other tragedies, where he believes in the eternal duration and the absolute stability of Zeus' rule.

Throughout the play Zeus is characterized as a tyrant. 'None is free except Zeus.' He is the new commander of the gods, a new master who, says the chorus of the Oceanids, 'with new-fangled laws holds lawless sway' – an illogical statement which is very much in the line of contemporary political criticism of tyranny. Aeschylus knew a tyrant, though a comparatively mild one, in Hiero of Syracuse; he eventually stayed at his court. Other statements are: 'It is the disease of tyranny to have no faith in friends'; 'To disregard the father's words is dangerous.' Zeus is a tyrant, and this is the one great problem for our understanding; for we know from other passages of Aeschylus that he believed in a just if powerful Zeus, a belief which even shows traces of monotheism. Is Zeus inscrutable, as Gilbert Murray thought, comparing him with the god of Job?

We also hear that Zeus intended to destroy all mankind and to create a new race of man. To the sympathetic chorus Prometheus speaks of what he himself has done for men. He took away from them the fear of death, he gave them hope, and by giving them fire, changed them from primitive cavemen into true human beings who knew about agriculture and breeding animals, knew how to read and to count, knew of medical help, etc. 'All arts came to men from Prometheus'; he was not the creator of 'culture', but of the inventive human mind. He assures the chorus that all this was done by him by his own will and in full knowledge of what was to happen to him as a punishment.

The situation is enlivened and at the same time more clearly characterized by two scenes; the first is the appearance of Okeanos. He comes as an old friend who wants to mediate. 'Know yourself' (the Delphic commonplace) and adapt yourself to the new tyrant. You have to learn humility. If Prometheus would express himself more mildly, Okeanos will try to plead for him. He is the type of opportunist elder statesman who once, with Prometheus, had helped Zeus. Prometheus treats him with manifest irony. In the end, Okeanos is easily persuaded not to endanger himself and to do nothing.

The other scene is that of Io, an innocent maiden with whom Zeus fell in love, causing the hatred of Hera. Changed into a cow and pursued by a gadfly, Io goes mad and flees all over the world. The story shows Zeus' cruel misuse of his power at its worst. Prometheus foretells her future: more wandering and suffering, and final peace when she gives birth to a son, a descendant of whom will liberate Prometheus. In half-disclosing his secret to Hermes, Zeus' callous servant, Prometheus brings final disaster upon himself. Under lightning and thunder, storm and earthquake, he sinks into Tartarus. But 'never will Zeus kill him' (1053). 'O holy mother, O aether revolving the common light to all, thou seest how unjustly I suffer' (1091 ff.). That is the end of the play. The Oceanids, the chorus of kind but playful and curious girls, refuse to leave him and also go down with him – an unexpected final event intended to win even more sympathy for Prometheus.

The second play of the trilogy was 'Prometheus Unbound'. We have only a number of fragments, some of them recent discoveries.

We hear of Prometheus' further punishments; the various stages are most likely Aeschylus' invention. After Tartarus he is chained on Causacus, and the eagle comes every day to eat from his liver, which grows again during the night. The immortal Prometheus is now longing for death. Then Heracles appears and shoots the eagle, hardly against the will of Zeus, though Prometheus addresses him as 'Dear son of a hostile father'. We hear that Zeus has made peace with Kronos, and has liberated the Titans who are now in Elysium. They form the chorus and pity their brother Prometheus, who is the only one left to oppose Zeus. There is an additional story: Zeus will only set Prometheus free if another god is willing to give up immortality and go to Hades; Chiron, who has an incurable wound and suffers great pains, is willing to go. All details and the real context are unknown, but Zeus had shown forgiveness to former enemies, and reconciliation seems in sight. One more point: as a result of Prometheus' liberation, men are ordered to wear festive crowns as a symbol of his chains. Was that an allusion to the Athenian festival, perhaps a prophecy? A third play followed, probably called *Pyrkaeus*, the fire-kindler, of which we know very little, though it is likely that it referred to the Athenian cult. Prometheus had brought the fire which was especially important for the potters and metal workers of Athens; they were the people involved in the Athenian worship of Prometheus. Like the *Eumenides* in the *Oresteia*, the final play would have brought full reconciliation, special praise for Athens and for Zeus as a god of grace and justice. But that is really only an assumption. We know nothing for certain.[2]

How did the change, both in Prometheus and Zeus, come about? That is a problem not finally solved. The extant tragedy has been called the tragedy of genius (W. Jaeger). But Prometheus is not a man nor is his work so general as sometimes assumed. He is a suffering god, and he suffered for his all-too-great love of man. Thus, he could become a symbol for Christianity, a Christ before

[2] [If the Prometheus plays were performed in Syracuse, possibly even after Aeschylus' death, it is not even certain that the trilogy was ever finished; cf. E. R. Dodds *The Ancient Concept of Progress* (1973), 37 ff.]

Christ. Tertullian calls Christ *verus Prometheus*. But that is quite unGreek. He is proud and prepared to suffer for what he thinks is right. He discloses his secret in the end, persuaded by his mother Gaia-Themis. We can only guess that Zeus' changed attitude played its part. Prometheus remains the heroic revolutionary.

The change in Zeus, if it is a change, is even more difficult to explain. Some scholars have spoken of a development in Zeus, and even compared the severe God of *Oedipus Rex* and the God of Grace in the New Testament. Zeus is called 'young' by Aeschylus, but that means 'new' because he has only recently gained his position. It does not mean that Zeus was young in the first play and older and wiser in the second and third. That is to say: there would have been no personal development, no moral transformation. We know that Aeschylus believed in Zeus as a great moral force. We have, for example, the hymn in *Agamemnon* (160 ff.): 'Zeus whoever he be . . . [a traditional way of saying whatever name he may like to be called], it is Zeus who has shown men the way to wisdom by establishing as a valid law "By suffering they will learn".' This is an old commonplace, but Aeschylus gives it deep religious and moral meaning, defining the relation between god and man. A few lines later, the song contains the formula 'violent grace' (*charis biaios*) which would cover Zeus' dual nature.[3]

It is certain that an earlier, more primitive tradition of the myth had some influence on Aeschylus, that the Greek picture of the gods had undergone changes. But I cannot believe that Aeschylus would ever depict a god developing from an earlier to a later stage. Greek gods did not develop, though they could have different aspects, different faces, and they might be different from men's changing beliefs.[4] Even Hesiod knows that Zeus combined both

[3] [Cf. K. Reinhardt *Eranos-Jahrbuch 1956* (25, 1957), 24 ff.; *Tradition u. Geist* (1960), 191 ff.; and H. Lloyd-Jones *The Justice of Zeus* (1971), 87 ff. He translates: 'a grace that comes by violence'. See also K. Reinhardt *Vermächtnis der Antike* (1960), 21.]

[4] [The change of the Erinyes into the Eumenides seems rather startling; but they remain essentially – apart from Athenian worship – still the same as before.]

power and justice, and the *Iliad* shows Zeus as a god of inner conflict who does not side with either the Greeks or the Trojans. Zeus
had not repented; the view of a development of his character is, I
believe, mistaken. Not he, but his position, has changed. His power
is no longer new, no longer disputed. When Prometheus says:
'But ever-ageing Time teaches all things', he does not refer to
evolution and development (ideas of the nineteenth and twentieth
centuries), but to a change in situation which causes different
reactions. Zeus has made some kind of settlement with Prometheus; he has made his peace with him, he no longer needs to be a
tyrant (he still could be if necessary). Zeus as the highest god of the
Greek polis is, for example, the protector of people who have been
wronged, as in Aeschylus' *Suppliants*. He could also be the god of
nature and as such either benevolent or destructive; we must not
forget the prevalent traditional idea of 'the envy of the gods'.
Aeschylus is not a critic of religion; he is deeply religious, but he
knows the paradox of God, the presence of both good and evil.
He is almost as much a thinker as a poet, and he knows about the
philosophical thought of his time, the conflict of contrasts and the
harmony deriving from that; witnesses are Heraclitus, Parmenides
and others. In the extant play the chorus speaks of the harmony of
Zeus, 'which men's counsels should never transgress'. That is a
hint at what later becomes manifest, but it is a fact which always was
and always will be true. The Greeks knew of no Satan, but there is
something Satanic in every Greek god.

We ought to add one more point. Stronger than all the
gods, stronger than Zeus, is Fate, Ananke or Moira, Necessity.
This knowledge is behind Prometheus' 'resignation' (if we may
call it that); he knows that neither he nor his great opponent
can ultimately act against Fate. All is predestined, and his
own achievements are nothing against Ananke. Prometheus has
often been taken as a symbol of the freedom of will. He is – to
a certain point. But ultimately the course of events is prefixed
by destiny. What is true of him, and even of Zeus, is of course
even more true of man. The so-called Prometheic attitude of
modern individualists and rebels has no real ancestor in the Greek
Prometheus.

However, the myth of Prometheus was immortal. He became a symbol for revolt against convention, for exuberant individualism, for man's fight against religious and political suppression.[5] That was not the Prometheus of the Greeks, though his figure contained the germs of the later picture. Moreover, in all that it must not be forgotten that above Prometheus and above Zeus there was the eternal power of fate. Prometheus fought a half-successful fight against fatalism. That is what makes him similar to, and at the same time distinguishes him from, Job.

I should like to end in a lighter vein. Aeschylus has also written a satyr drama (the comic final play after three tragedies), probably called *Prometheus Pyrkaeus*, the fire-kindler, known only by a few fragments in which the satyrs see fire for the first time and in their delight burn their beards. Prometheus also appears in one of Aristophanes' comedies, *The Birds*. Peithetaerus has founded his city between Earth and Heaven, and thus has deprived the gods of the burnt offerings of men. Therefore there is war between Olympus and Cloudcuckoobury. Prometheus, heavily disguised, visits Peithetaerus in order to tell him about the situation of the gods. But what a Prometheus! Terribly afraid that Zeus might see him, he asks Peithetaerus to hold an umbrella over him so that Zeus will not discover him. And then he discloses: 'It's all over with Zeus.' The gods are starving. Prometheus speaks of envoys that will come down to negotiate with Peithetaerus and prepares him for that: 'Make no peace unless the Birds gain again full freedom and you will be given Basileia (Sovereignty) as a wife.' Peithetaerus asks what sort of a woman she is, and is told: a lovely girl who is in charge of Zeus' laws, of good order, and of common sense. Naturally, Peithetaerus is delighted. The final exchanges are:

Prometheus: 'You know I am always well-disposed to men.'

Peithetaerus: 'Aye, but for you we could not fry our fish.'

Prometheus: 'And I hate every god, as you know well ... But

---

[5] [I have not seen: R. Trousson *Le Thème de Prométhée dans la littérature européenne* (1964), 2 vols.]

it's time to go. Let's have the umbrella; then if Zeus sees me from above he will think I am following the Panathenaic procession.'

It was, ever since Homer, a privilege of the Greeks that they could make fun of their gods. But the original myth and its very nature shines through fun and satire. The same is true of Zeus and the other gods; they have human qualities even though they are far more powerful than men.

4

Dike and Eros[1]

One of the reproaches made against Classical scholars, and one
which derives from love for the Classics not from dislike or lack of
understanding, is more justifiable and goes nearer to the core of
the matter than probably any other. We are reproached with the
fact that in spite of all the learned scholarship of many generations,
there are very few books which, pleasantly but not superficially,
provide the reader who is not a scholar with a description of essential features of antiquity. It is claimed that we who are always
thinking and talking of the eternal values of the Classics fail to
make them come alive now. In the past scholars were outstripped
by lay writers of books which were widely read by the general
public. The result was that the public frequently received very ingenious speculations or fanciful pictures of the ancient world, but
learned very little, if anything, of its true nature. Since very few
writers have intuitive genius, it is chiefly by strict and accurate
scholarship that the truth, or at least something near to it, can be
recovered. And yet how very few books are learned enough and at
the same time interesting enough to enable the common reader to
realize the truth about ancient times – which, we agree, is of funda-

[1] Translated from a review of Sven Lönborg's *Dike und Eros. Menschen und
Mächte im alten Athen* (1924), published in the *Frankfurter Zeitung* (4 March
1925).

mental importance for modern men and women who claim to be, or want to become, cultured people. It seems worth while to remember a book practically unknown today. The book, translated from Swedish and published in German almost fifty years ago, provides exactly what we need for a limited though outstanding period of the history of the Greek mind; it raises questions old and new. The author is Swedish, and I must confess that I do not know whether he is a professional scholar or an amateur; but he has acquired wide knowledge and has obviously had a really scholarly education. He is, at any rate, the right mixture, even though we cannot always follow him. His book, which deserves a translation into English, is one of the rare works which are destined to keep alive the legacy of the Classical Age better than all preaching about the values of humanism. Round the three centres of Pericles the Statesman, Euripides the Poet and Socrates the Sage, the Athens of the Great War is visualized and, as it were, restored. This Athens is in the process of changing from the old city of those who fought at Marathon and from the State of Pericles and Sophocles, to the city which, while politically living on the heritage of the past, brought forth the greatest revelations of Greek thought.

An introductory chapter describes the city itself, and at the same time brings the historical events down to the moment when Pericles begins his career. A portrait of the statesman follows. All educated people have in their mind some conception, however stereotyped, of Pericles as a great democrat and a great patron of the fine arts. In this book an attempt is made to understand the politician – and that means, in fact, the man as a whole – as an exponent of developments which were chiefly determined by spiritual ideas. Mr Lönborg goes so far as to declare that it was Pericles' aim from the beginning of his career to create in the world of reality one of those ideal states which from the fifth century onwards became one of the central subjects of philosophical discussion. This is undoubtedly an exaggeration – perhaps less if applied to the finished statesman, but certainly if applied to the 'party-leader' Pericles was at first. Yet the over-statement reveals one essential side of Pericles' true nature. We shall not understand him unless we realize that his whole mind was dominated by philosophical ideas – as Plutarch says, of his rhetoric alone, that 'natural philosophy (*physiologia*) was poured out over it like a dye'. According to Mr Lönborg, Pericles was the exponent of 'a democratic policy of ideas' such as was never accomplished anywhere else. Every democratic leader, however, if he is truly both a democrat and a leader, faces the fundamental problem which Thucydides has summed up with regard to Pericles in the famous statement that Athens, 'though in name a democracy, was in fact ruled by her greatest man'. The problem of democratic leadership has, necessarily, implications which may prove tragic. Lönborg only touches on them very lightly and hardly mentions Pericles' relations to Athena, who was for him a symbol of the greatness of Athens and at the same time the ruling goddess of the people's religion.

Euripides, in Lönborg's opinion, is Athens' greatest poet. About this superlative it is easy to quarrel. Our generation, on the whole, is inclined to put the 'titanism' of Aeschylus far above the theatrical genius of Euripides. Mr Lönborg repeats the comparison of Euripides with Ibsen, which has become fairly common, though it narrows too much the scope of Euripides' mind. Although it does not do justice to the Greek dramatist (who was as clever as Ibsen both as a playwright and a social critic, but greater as an artist), the comparison makes it very clear why we are conscious of Euripides' limitations rather than of his greatness, of his theatre rather than of his art, of his reasoning rather than of his searching philosophy. It is only too likely that our verdict will be in the end as unjust as the opposite view, and, if we follow Lönborg in getting rid of the fetters of conventional aesthetics, we shall be better able to realize the tragic greatness of Euripides' humanity, which permeates his work even where it looks at first sight rationalist or rhetorical.[2]

Mr Lönborg, in analysing a large number of Euripides' plays, does not simply tell us the plot nor does he criticize the structure. Writing without any pretension to philosophical aesthetics he works out, by a method of immediate, almost personal, approach,

---

[2] [A new estimation of Euripides has been started with E. R. Dodds' article on 'Euripides the Irrationalist' (*Cl. Rev.* 43, 1929, 97 ff. = *The Ancient Concept of Progress*, 1973, 78 ff.)]

the peculiarities of manner and matter of each play, and makes the stories live again. The plays are depicted against the contemporary background of political events and intellectual trends. Probably the most striking example of the mutual connections which existed between tragedy and life, between the poet and his surroundings, is the following. At the Dionysia of 415 B.C., when the Sicilian expedition was being prepared, *The Trojan Women* was performed as the last of three Trojan plays. The prophetic poet described, in the irresponsibility of Paris and the disaster of Troy, the irresponsibility of Alcibiades and its gravest consequence, the terrible disaster at Syracuse, which actually happened more than two years later. Lönborg reproduces this tragedy of Euripides in a manner which reveals that, though a neutral during the war, he shared to the full the deep and stirring experience of the suffering and the tragic disasters of peoples and individuals. In a way he went through something similar to the experience of the Austrian poet Franz Werfel, who wrote before the First World War a tragedy which was half a translation and half a transformation of the same play of Euripides.

This is one of the high spots in Lönborg's record of Euripides; the other one is the description of the *Bacchae*. Euripides, who left Athens for Macedon before he wrote this play, has moved away from the problems of the day to become – in a purer sense than perhaps in any of his earlier plays – the 'poet'. He remains, however, always the 'thinker'. It is important to realize that Euripides, who reflects so much of the reasoning of his age, does so not because of a naturalistic tendency, that is in order to imitate life, nor, on the other hand, to expound his own philosophy. And yet he is with full intention a teacher of his people. As Mr Lönborg puts it, 'he brings "men" and "movements" to face one another in such a way that every spectator recognized a problem which he had to solve for himself'. And the 'movement' meant the Dionysus cult which was fully alive, whether at Athens or in Macedon, in those days. Euripides stands on the borderline between poet and philosopher. He derives his creative power largely from that didactic urge which is equally important, although it appears in different ways, in every one of the great tragedians, but finds its culminating expression in the man whom the Delphic god called the wisest of all men.

The third and largest section of Lönborg's book is dedicated to Socrates. Everybody knows that the Athenian sage is the philosopher who never wrote anything, and whom we know only from the descriptions of his disciples; even they did not intend to give an impartial and objective 'historical' picture of their beloved master. It is equally well known that Socrates became one of the most disputed figures in the history of the human mind. In his picture, as it is reflected throughout the ages, all imaginable shades and colours occur, the two extremes being the enlightened rationalist and the prophet 'drunk with the god'. Lönborg can neglect all these attempts to systematize and classify the enigmatic sage because he does not intend to add a new attempt to their number. The goal of what is commonly called the Socratic philosophy is to Lönborg 'not the art of discussing notions, but the art of life'. This conclusion has been drawn before, though usually not by philosophers. The personal and outstanding achievement of Lönborg lies in his ability to put in the place of the general statement a picture of a living man.

It is significant that he begins with the pleasant anecdote recorded by Xenophon that Socrates once told the hetaera Theodote that he knew better than she how to make friends. This story, together with several of Plato's dialogues, is used to demonstrate that Socrates – particularly in using his famous irony – aimed only at inducing people to think about themselves and to examine themselves. This becomes the criterion which helps to distinguish between Socratic and Platonic methods. It is not an absolutely certain criterion, but the same can be said of all other attempts to draw the line of demarcation between the great master and his great pupil. With the same special talent which is revealed in Lönborg's manner of introducing us to Euripides' plays, the contents of those dialogues of Plato from which we can learn to understand the historical Socrates are now reproduced. The author pleads, with fairly good reasons though not entirely convincingly, for the inclusion not only of the early works of Plato but also, and in particular, of the dialogues which belong to the period of his ripeness, such as *Phaedrus* and *Symposium*. Beyond the methods of Socrates, which are themselves more than mere methods, the whole essence of Socrates' nature as a man and a thinker is depicted. We come to understand his relations with the youth of Athens, with the state, the gods and the Sophists. We may sometimes have our doubts whether it is fully justifiable to use as evidence this or that sentence of Plato's or this or that story from Xenophon; but the result as a whole remains unshaken. We are given a complete and detailed picture of the unique man who became the father of European philosophy, not because he was the first philosopher but because he was the first to show how to philosophize.

Mr Lönborg's book, of which I have given here only a brief résumé that is in no way adequate, is written with love and enthusiasm, and it ought to be read in the same spirit. As far as possible he lets the Greeks speak with their own words. Although he (or rather his translator) has not always used the best available translations and sometimes misses the point of the original, the way he conceals himself behind the men whom he describes, and behind their utterances, is exemplary. I said 'behind the *men*' – but title and subtitle promise more. 'Men and Movements', 'Dike and Eros' – where do they come in? The first phrase is a rather inadequate translation of the German expression, and the second is very difficult to translate at all: 'Justice and Love' is probably the nearest thing we can find though it is not satisfactory. In fact, an ambitious programme is expressed by these titles, and the book does not fully live up to it. The author writes almost exclusively about men, not movements; about individuals, not the ideas behind them. *Dike* and *Eros* are the mighty powers – and 'powers' is actually the word used in the subtitle – which have built the Greek state on the foundation of justice, and shaped man from the wealth of love. Together they are the forces through which both state and man are supposed to find perfection. We may be able to trace even in Lönborg's book these forces behind the men. But the author never speaks of them expressly, and the reader has to supply more than can reasonably be expected of him. He must know something of that divine Dike, that idea of right and justice, with which Hesiod challenged his greedy and unjust brother, and which was also the basis on which Solon stood when he struggled against the extremists on both sides. It was Dike which opened the door of politics to the lower classes, and it was also Dike for which the Greeks fought against Persian despotism. It is the divine Dike who in the plays of the great tragedians triumphs over *hubris*, human insolence and pride, and it is Dike which as τὸ δίκαιον becomes the signpost leading to the ultimate good, Plato's god. If Dike shaped the body and mind of Greek life, Eros shaped its soul. If Dike led the way in politics and ethics, Eros led in the relationship between human beings and in creative art. Nothing in Lönborg's book alludes to all this, but I believe that he has fused into one the meaning of title and subtitle and the contents of the book, if not in his words, at least in his thoughts. We realize – and this is the ultimate result of our reading – that it was the statesman and poet who struggled for the proclamation and realization of Dike; while the sage, going beyond this, owed final wisdom to his deepest emotion, to Eros. Both words are personifications, but as such they are gods, and they bridge the gulf between man and man as well as between man's community and the gods.[3]

[3] [Since this paper was written much more has been said on Classical Athens. Even more important, the position of the Classics in our society has greatly changed. But I feel Lönborg's book may still be relevant today.]

5

Some aspects of the transition from the Classical to the Hellenistic Age[1]

The transition which is the subject of this talk is a very complex phenomenon, as is, in fact, any transition between two periods of history. Old and New, tradition and individual achievement, destruction and creation, all are combined. In a way, of course, all history is history in transition, but only in a way, for the essential things are those which are not transitory. They are those having a life in their own right, though it may happen that they also belong to two periods, and thus have a share in the process of transition; we shall see an example of that later. With regard to our particular epoch, there was much in the world of fifth- and fourth-century Greece that prepared for the great changes ahead, and what is true of Greece can also be maintained of the Persian empire, of Asia Minor, of Egypt. Everywhere during that time there were possible nuclei of a new phase of history. And yet, they would have had little, or at the most a rather delayed, effect if Alexander had not done what so often is the task of the genius: to make the decisive break and to anticipate centuries of future history. Alexander did, in a sense, the same as Caesar did, and his aims were equally superseded by a more fragmentary, though more gradual and more organic, development in which the bridges to the past were still

[1] Unpublished lecture delivered at Columbia and Princeton Universities in 1958.

52

used for some time and those into the future were only slowly built.

These general remarks, which (you will be pleased to hear) I do not intend to go on with, are merely made in order to give a kind of background to particular problems, and to protect me against the complaint of neglecting the wider picture. I am going to deal with one or perhaps two special aspects, but first I must admit that I was roused to start on this subject by the impression I got from an article by a scholar whom I esteem very highly, but whose views in this case I found completely unconvincing. Thus this paper today is largely polemical. What I really should like very much would be to have a debate on the suggestions or counter-suggestions which I have to make. My views are unimportant, but the historical questions involved are, I think, quite important.

Among the historical phenomena which bridge the gap between the Classical era of Greece and the Hellenistic Age, the one belonging to, and of outstanding importance in, either period is the polis. It is true that 'polis' is a word with many different meanings; its etymology is uncertain, even the most accurate Greek writers could use it for a walled city, for its acropolis, for Sparta that had no walls, for cities Greek and non-Greek, for states with an urban centre and sometimes (though rarely) even for states without that if they played a similar part in Greek politics. A polis usually had a founder, whether mythical or real, whether god or hero; it aimed at independence, at freedom and autonomy, but did not always completely possess it. Ought we, as has sometimes been suggested, give up using the word at all? I do not think so. We need this kind of abstraction in order not to lose ourselves in the jungle of details and differences. The use of our word 'state' is even more ambiguous and varied. And yet we cannot do without the word or the concept.

It is a legitimate question to ask to what extent the Classical polis – the Athens, Sparta, Corinth, Syracuse, etc., of the fifth and fourth centuries, one type of state despite all differences – survived into the new era to play a new important part in it. We must not, of course, forget that concepts like 'the Classical polis' and 'the Hellenistic polis' are also abstractions, and that there were in either period very many poleis different to a point in structure and composition.

Again we are justified in using the abstractions in order to see the wood and not only the trees. In general, it can probably be said that the Hellenistic polis in its internal structure shared most of the constitutional features of the Classical polis, while the surroundings, the relations to the outer world, were for most of them completely different. Without a doubt, the nature of the Hellenistic polis, the varieties of its constitution and its relations to the rulers of the time, are a very complex question for which, moreover, evidence is scanty and haphazard. The minds of scholars have become rather heated over these problems, and any attempt at drawing a general picture (as for example that by A. H. M. Jones in his *The Greek City from Alexander to Justinian*) has met and will meet with the criticism of those who may have found faults and oversights or discovered some inscriptions which do not fit into the general picture. We must realize that some of the necessary alterations and qualifications will be very important indeed.

Recently Professor Bradford Welles, an outstanding expert on Hellenistic inscriptions and on the Hellenistic polis, has written an article also called 'The Greek City', in which he rightly points out some of the questions involved.[2] In trying to bridge the gulf (or we may say: the alleged gulf) between the Classical and the Hellenistic polis he admits the great difficulty caused by the lack of 'the necessary detailed information about any Hellenistic city'. It does not provide a solution when Mlle Préaux in an otherwise very helpful paper tries to use the unique and peculiar draft of the constitution of Cyrene under the first Ptolemy as a guide for the late polis generally.[3] It is however certain, especially after some of the detailed research of Louis Robert, that, on the one hand, there can be no single formula covering all the constitutional variations; on the other hand, we can see that not only the purely Greek cities, say, round the shores of Asia Minor, but also the Hellenized cities (we know now of a great number of small and unimportant places in the interior of Asia Minor and elsewhere) use (to quote Robert *La Carie* II, 300) 'the forms and the spirit of the political life' traditionally connected with the polis. Without denying the possibility of

[2] *Studi in Onore di Calderini e Paribeni* I (1956), 81 ff.
[3] *Les villes hellénistiques*, etc. (*Recueil de la Soc. J. Bodin*, 1954, 1956.)

occasional variations, we can be practically sure that all the Hellenistic poleis had their assembly, council, and annual officials. When Delphi (*Syll.* 548, about 211 B.C.) grants to the polis or the demos of Sardes and her envoys *proxenia, promanteia, ateleia,* etc., thus *expressis verbis* renewing an old relationship going back to Croesus, this need not mean (as Welles shows against Jones) that it implies a formal recognition of Sardes as a Greek city; but it does mean recognition as a polis, Greek or otherwise; to deny this means contradicting the words of the inscription as well as those of a later one (*OGI* 305, c. 167 B.C.) where we read that Sardes has sent ambassadors with an official *psephisma.* I believe we must accept the variety as well as the unity of the concept of the Hellenistic polis and its close links with the Classical polis. In special aspects, as for example that of law, the continuity is obvious.[4] There was a spreading extension of the polis, geographically and ethnically, but there was no fundamental break in its history, and no gulf existed that had to be bridged.

You may think this is to some extent vague and general, though it is supported by a good deal of occasional and dispersed evidence. Anyway, the crucial period is the fourth century. It has long been known that monarchy made its reappearance at that time, that rulers such as Dionysius and Maussolus can be regarded as predecessors of the Hellenistic kings. This is, it might be said, confined to the more marginal regions of the Greek world, regions under the shadow of foreign powers, Carthage or Persia, and it was also in a marginal country that the prevailing monarchy of the Macedons became part of Greek politics. What about Athens, the centre of the Greek mind? Democracy did not allow for any form of monarchy; but if there was no practical possibility, what about the theory of monarchy? It is here that Professor Welles found his starting point from which he developed a new and surprising theory of the influence of the political theorists on the shape of things to come, that is to say, of monarchy as well as the later polis. Thus, not only Isocrates (the favourite pawn for some time past in this game) but also Plato and Aristotle appear as the main pillars of the bridge Welles wishes to build. His argument culminates in the startling

[4] Cf., e.g., Cl. Préaux, *Chronique d'Egypte* (1958).

statement: 'The Hellenistic monarchy was not created by Philip or Alexander or their successors, it was created by Greek theoreticians and publicists; it was not designed to extinguish the Greek city but to preserve it.'

Whatever is right or wrong in this statement, two things, I feel, are mixed up which have to be distinguished: Hellenistic monarchy and the Hellenistic polis. Whatever the ancestry of either of them, I hope to be able to show that it cannot have been one and the same. I believe there is simply no substance in the idea that Hellenistic monarchy was intended for either preserving or extinguishing the polis. We shall try to find out whether in theory there was a connection between the two. In practice they became involved, and very closely indeed, with one another, but monarchy arose independently. None of the kings, neither the king of the Macedonians nor those who ruled in Asia and Egypt, ever thought of the polis as anything else but an instrument of their imperial policy. It was in many ways a necessary instrument (though much less so in Egypt than elsewhere), but the fact and the nature of the new form of state, of the territorial monarchy, emerged without any design for the future of the polis, except that, one way or another, it had to be made part of the realm. In the growth of these realms and their inner coherence the poleis were to be of greatest importance. The civilization of the Hellenistic Age would not have been what it was without the polis, but that is quite a different matter.

We shall now briefly discuss the evidence from the philosophers, first with regard to the nature of the polis. In *The Republic* Plato shows the needs of man from which the polis arises. That may be called 'a functional, not a formal concept', but that is so because Plato only wishes gradually to build up his own state. The polis of Utopia, whatever Plato may have thought of its practical possibilities, was no model for real use. It seems to be different with the *Laws*. There we are on firmer ground. In general, Plato's works were widely read in Hellenistic times; they influenced some of the Eastern, especially Jewish writers until eventually Philo emerged, who has been called the Jewish Plato. But this widespread knowledge of Plato is least true of the *Laws*, of which W. Jaeger says that it found in antiquity no interpreters and few readers. Welles, on the other hand, maintains that 'the *Laws* provides a useful background for the urbanising activity of the Hellenistic kings, for it was certainly well known to them and their advisers'. The word 'certainly' is a dangerous word; I fear we all use it too easily when there is no evidence. As the clever schoolboy explains: 'An axiom is a thing so visible that there is no need to see it.' I have the greatest doubts whether any of the Macedonian generals and kings, even a cultured man like Philadelphos or the genuine Stoic Antigonos Gonatas, would have bothered reading that lengthy and partly very boring work. As to their advisers, we simply cannot know; but there is, I believe, no sign of any philosophical mind being employed in the tasks of founding and organizing the Hellenistic empires and cities. The task of Demetrius of Phaleron in Alexandria was of a completely different kind.

Naturally, any description of an imaginary and ideal foundation like that of the Magnetes in the *Laws* would contain features which could be applied to other foundations. All the details mentioned by Welles of site and size, of voluntary settlers, of the agrarian basis, of the social structure, of education of the citizens, do not prove more than that Plato built his ideal state upon the realities of Greek political life. His citizens are directed by their officials and the nocturnal Council, to be trained as members of a well and meticulously ordered community; they were not to be disturbed by other activities in their aiming at the εὖ ζῆν. Thus, agricultural work (although Plato is not quite explicit about that), commerce, manufacture, and any lower services were to be performed by metics and slaves. This, of course, is neither a new nor an unusual idea in Greek political theory. It had even a certain foundation in reality. The economic activities of metics and slaves in fourth-century Athens, although sometimes exaggerated, were of great importance. The part played by serfs and *perioeci* in states such as Sparta, Crete and Thessaly is well known, and in Greek poleis in Asia Minor the natives in the surrounding countryside had always been a working non-citizen population. When Alexander in some of his foundations – from the first Alexandria to Alexandria Eschate – let non-Greeks join in the settlement, this did not necessarily go beyond common Greek practice. It is true, we hear that in Alexandria

Eschate he made natives full citizens; if so, he acted according to the urgent necessities of the situation, and at the same time following his own ideas (so alien to the polis and its theorists) about the fusion of races, especially Greeks and Iranians. That, by the way, is something different from the idea of the brotherhood of man; as to that, I share the scepticism of many scholars whether Alexander's policy was ever dominated by it. Alexander was not in need of any theoretical model, and he certainly did nothing to prevent those Greeks and Macedonians whom he settled in foreign lands from working on the land or doing business, though he naturally regarded them in the first instance as the defenders of the city. We ought to think of the part played by military settlers everywhere in Hellenistic times in order to realize that agriculture and military service very often went hand in hand.

Plato's second-best state was an ingenious mixture of Athenian, Spartan, Cretan and Platonic features. It was an agrarian community shaped by a combination of ethical and aesthetic ideas; and with its negation of trade and manufacture, its narrowness and primitivity, was in complete contrast to the economic ideas of the Hellenistic Age. There can be no doubt that the detailed institutions as foreseen by the Athenian stranger teach us a great deal about the workings of a polis. But the separation of theory from practice is uncertain and difficult, and so much that is taken from real life, just because it was there, could be known from the usual practice in many poleis. In fact, Welles discovers only one important similarity between the city of the Magnetes and the average Hellenistic polis, and that is that neither of the two had any real foreign policy. But the neglect of foreign policy by the political theorists is a well-known fact, occasionally criticized though hardly overcome by Aristotle. Certainly, this negative fact could not be of any help for understanding the Hellenistic polis, and it is a bold *tour de force* to argue that, though the Magnesians were not expected to live under the rule of a king, the lack of foreign policy would enable them to do so.

If we cannot accept Plato's polis or any other philosophical ideal as a model for the Hellenistic polis, we must still ask to what extent the monarchy of the later age was foreshadowed by Greek philosophers and writers. Nobody can doubt that during the fourth century the idea of monarchy made some progress among the Greeks. The picture of a well-trained single ruler appealed to the minds of those who abhorred democracy and at the same time believed in education. A whole new branch of literature developed, based on the idea that it might be possible to educate a monarch and in that way achieve an ideal form of state. It began with Xenophon's pedagogic fantasy, the *Cyropaideia*, which had nothing to do with Persia but everything with a Greek ideal. There are other examples during the fourth century, though all set in the colonial world, outside the fixed polis tradition of the motherland.

Plato, in theory and, we may say, also in practice, namely in his Sicilian adventure, was thinking in terms of philosopher kings. Their rule represents the best possible constitution, that of a tyrant the worst. The more astonishing seems a passage in the *Laws* (709E). A question is put to the imaginary lawgiver about what kind of polis he wants to deal with, and he replies: 'Give me a Polis ruled by a tyrant, though the tyrant must be young, with a good memory, well educated, manly and with a magnificent nature.' What is the meaning of this passage? A salvation of tyranny? That is most unlikely. Clearly, that paragon of virtue was very different from the usual, and also from Plato's usual idea of a tyrant. Moreover, he was only to serve, as it were, as an instrument. He was supposed to agree with a great legislator; that is to say, he would be under the law and thus no tyrant at all. The point in question is once more the ability of the ruler to be or to become a philosopher. Perhaps, when Plato wrote these lines, the memory of the idealized picture of the younger Dionysios which he had once cherished was still, if unconsciously, in his mind. The description, originally given by Dion, of Dionysios' character (Plat. *ep.* 7, 328A) is in very similar terms, and so was to some extent the information which induced Plato to undertake his second journey (339B). The seeming inconsistency of the passage mentioned is largely an inconsistency of expression. Plato did not wish to praise tyranny, rather (as on a lower level Isocrates did in his Nicocles speeches) to legalize it and thus to use the monarch as an executive for the building of his own foundation.

Moreover, whatever form of monarchy he may have extolled,

here or elsewhere, as for example in the 'royal man' ($\beta\alpha\sigma\iota\lambda\iota\kappa\delta s$ $\dot{\alpha}\nu\dot{\eta}\rho$) in his *Politikos*, it was – as with Aristotle – a kingdom within the polis, and an ideal polis at that. In the case of Aristotle, it was not even monarchy alone, but aristocracy as well. Those one or few who are so full of virtue, of *aretê*, that they stand out far above their fellow citizens, can no longer be regarded as part of the state. The two chief passages in Aristotle's *Politics* (1228 a, 15 and 1284, 3) culminate in the famous words: 'Such a man will naturally be like a god among men'. Is this really, as Welles maintains, 'the fully developed theoretical basis of the Hellenistic monarchy, complete with ruler cult?' Many years ago I tried to show that it is nothing of the kind.[5] I repeat the most important arguments and will try to put them on firmer foundations. First, Aristotle speaks of aristocracy as well as of monarchy. Secondly, the phrase 'like a god among men' was a conventional idiom, used before by poets and writers without the slightest indication of rulership or ruler cult. I refer to passages which represent the more important part of the evidence available. A very complete survey (with not always convincing interpretations) is given by Taeger in his important book *Charisma* (1957). The tradition, you see, goes back to Homer, and can then be traced down to the fourth century, a tradition not only of a certain idea but even of its wording. The passage of the *Iliad* (24, 258) is from Priam's angry speech to his surviving sons when he laments the dead; god-like Mestor, the charioteer Troilus, and above all Hector 'who was a god among men and seemed not like a mortal's son, but the son of a god'. This is the only passage in Homer, as far as I know, which does not say $\dot{\omega}s$ $\theta\epsilon\dot{o}s$; it means identity rather than similarity with the deity. We shall see that actually this difference makes little difference in the later tradition. Hector was dead, but I do not think that Priam's words are in the manner of a dirge and therefore do not mean that a living man is called a god. They *do* mean that, for they remember Hector as he was alive. Still, in the whole *Iliad* Hector is never anything but a great *man*. The verse shows (as later evidence confirms) that the phrase $\theta\epsilon\dot{o}s$ $\mu\epsilon\tau'$ $\dot{\alpha}\nu\delta\rho\dot{\alpha}\sigma\iota\nu$ (or similar) is simply a way of praising a man above his fellow men, possible also because Homer's gods are

[5] *Alexander and the Greeks* (1938), ch. 3.

often, in fact, only all-too-human. That exactly, and nothing else, is also the meaning in other passages. What was said of Hector, Theognis (339) says of himself: friend among friends, and stronger than his enemies, he would feel to be a god among men – provided he would not succumb to death. This is anything but a case of deification; he is a mortal in fear of death. A fragment from Eupolis' *Demoi* (117K) speaks of the Athenian *strategi* 'to whom we prayed as to gods, and they actually were' (we must assume: gods). And the *citharoedes* of Middle Comedy (Antiphanes, frag. 209K) is a god among men because he knows his art so well. Can it be shown more clearly that we have here a conventional form of praise? Plato (who in other passages often speaks of the divine man or similar forms) deals with the effects of the invisibility granted by Gyges' ring when a man can do what he likes without being made responsible (*Rep.* 360 B.C.); he is godlike (a common concept), but the words ἐν τοῖς ἀνθρώποις are a reminder that the passage refers to our traditional formula. A variation is also Alexander's famous utterance (Plut. *Alex.* 51 ff.) about the Greeks compared with the Macedonians as demigods among animals, a variation which again strongly confirms the original phrase as a well-known idiom. Isocrates (9, 72) tells us quite plainly that the words in question are a hyperbolic, chiefly poetical phrase. That is quite likely; but we can explain it as the result of a common Greek attitude. While on the one hand the Greeks believe (as most strikingly Pindar did) that man is separated from the gods by a deep unbridgeable gulf, namely his mortality, the wish, on the other hand, to be like a god and the tendency to describe an outstanding person in terms of divinity, even to worship a man who may be especially wonderful or powerful or helpful, these tendencies were always strong and always in the Greek mind. The same, I believe, is also behind the famous passage in Isocrates' letter to Philip (*epist.* 3, 5) when he writes that after full victory over Persia 'nothing will be left to you but to become a god'. Are we to think that Philip was deeply impressed by this compliment? Or that Isocrates regarded Philip's deification as a serious possibility? I very much doubt either view. To be sure, there were cults of Philip, and Professor Momigliano in his *Philippo il Macedone* has collected much evidence, though most of it is later and proves little, if anything, for the living Philip. Still I am not going to deny that in some Greek communities Philip became an object of religious worship, and still less that in utterances like that of Isocrates an attitude of mind is reflected that would easily admit the idea of ruler cult. There can be no doubt that some of its foundations were Greek.

Isocrates was a good patriot, first as an Athenian and then as a Greek. How strong his influence was outside his immediate pupils, we cannot say, probably neither so far-reaching nor so negligible as some modern scholars believe. In many ways he was an opportunist. The one idea which runs through his life and writing from the *Panegyrikos* to the *Philippos* is that of an Hellenic war against Persia. But that idea was in the air, and it is very doubtful whether Philip and Alexander in their political plans were particularly impressed by the old man's pamphlets. His views regarding the treatment of the barbarians which in 346 he described as in need of liberation and Greek protection, but after 338 as suited to serve the Greeks as helots, were perhaps a little less narrow than those of Aristotle – at least, that Aristotle who gave Alexander the advice to treat the Greeks as friends but the barbarians like animals or plants – but even Isocrates' views did not have any real effect on later monarchies. Isocrates and Aristotle probably did even less in preparing the Hellenistic monarchy than Cicero did in preparing Augustus' principate. The modern mind (I know because I have done the same more than once) is all too easily inclined to see ideas as the forerunners of events; sometimes it may be the other way round.

Welles made the philosophers of the fourth century, including Isocrates, the missing link between the Classical and the Hellenistic polis. I have tried to show that his arguments were unsound. Plato and Aristotle in their political writings essentially looked backwards, and the real trends of contemporary history evaded them. The ideal state, Utopia, the state without place on earth, was a flight from reality, however deeply its roots were embedded in the soil of the polis. As to Isocrates, his political ideas were largely based on emotional and human concepts such as *eunoia* and *homonoia* which were to rule the relations between man and man. As a true pupil of the sophists, Isocrates had a firm belief in man, but his ideas – like those of the philosophers – remained confined to an intellectual minority. As such they were important and might have influenced the thought of the Hellenistic Age, but their impact in the sphere of political reality was negligible.

Hellenistic monarchy drew its strength to some extent from Greek individualism and Greek theory, but far stronger was the bond to the Macedonian and Oriental traditions of monarchy. The Hellenistic polis traced its nature from that of the old polis, adapting itself or being adapted to new conditions without essentially altering its structure. The one new and real problem concerned relations between polis and monarchy. Each side needed the other, and had therefore to find a *modus vivendi*. And they did find it, not as one fixed solution, but in various ways according to the situation. Still, that is a different subject, outside our task today.

6

The Hellenistic Age[1]

I. INTRODUCTION

The Hellenistic Age, by almost general consent, covers the period
from 323 to 30 B.C.; i.e. from the death of Alexander the Great to
the incorporation of Egypt in the Roman empire. The concept of
this period as having a character all its own is not older than the
early nineteenth century, when the German historian J. G. Droysen
realized the cultural unity behind the history of a number of states.
He used the word *Hellenismus* as the name for an age which he
regarded as the transitional period between Classical Greece and
the Christian world; he forgot the part played by Rome, but nevertheless he had discovered an historical truth of the greatest importance.

As with most historical periods, the exact time limits are artificial, but though they may be due to convention they make sense.
Alexander's exploits had changed the face of the world, and from
the break-up of his empire there arose the numerous monarchies,
most of them ruled by Macedonians, which covered the eastern
Mediterranean and the Near East and were the framework for the
spread of Greek culture, the mixture of Greek and non-Greek populations and the fusion of Greek and Eastern elements. Thus, though
it is possible to speak of men and features as forerunners of the

[1] © 1964 by *Encyclopaedia Britannica*, and reprinted by permission.

Hellenistic Age and some historians took the middle of the fourth century as the beginning of the new era, the beginning of the new epoch in 323 B.C. can be regarded as established. It is less obvious with the date of 30 B.C. The three centuries of the Hellenistic Age were at the same time the period of the glory and decline of the Roman Republic. From the beginning of the second century B.C. the Hellenistic world came under increasing pressure from Rome, the interconnection between the two historical worlds grew in intensity and the main Hellenistic powers were entirely absorbed one after another. The conquest of Egypt by Octavian (later the emperor Augustus) was the last of these Roman victories.

On the other hand, it has been maintained that the first three centuries A.D. still belong to the Hellenistic Age because many Hellenistic cultural phenomena, especially the intermixture between West and East, continued and in some respects even grew in historical significance. In a sense the Hellenistic Age found its final continuation in the civilization of Byzantium. However, the mere fact of the unification of the *oecumene* ('the inhabited world') under Rome, the disappearance of the Hellenistic States, the establishment of the Pax Romana and the influence of the Latin language and of Roman law and administration fundamentally changed the Hellenistic world. It is right to distinguish between the Hellenistic Age of the last three centuries B.C. and the Greco-Roman civilization of the Imperial Age.

The word Hellenistic derives from the Greek word *hellenizein*, which in ancient times simply meant 'to speak Hellenic' (i.e. Greek) or 'to act like a Greek'. It could be used for either Greeks or non-Greeks in the sense of speaking correct Greek, but it was mainly used with regard to non-Greeks who had accepted the Greek way of life. The corresponding noun could occasionally be used in the sense of 'imitation of the Greeks'. In modern times Hellenism has become an ambiguous word, implying Greek culture as well as its imitation; in English, its use is not confined to the Hellenistic era, but often refers to enthusiasm for the art, literature and philosophy of Classical Greece (sometimes even involving lack of sympathy with the Hellenistic Age proper), particularly in the eighteenth and nineteenth centuries. J. G. Droysen used the word chiefly to indicate the fusion of East and West, and to a large extent this is indeed the essence of the period. Modern research has tended towards the view that the Greeks rather than the East were the contributing side. It will be seen that such a view, however justifiable in many respects, is too sweeping to do justice to the multifarious pattern of Hellenistic life. But at least it makes sense to call an age 'Hellenistic' of which the spreading of Greek civilization was a main feature. The *oecumene* was to a large extent hellenized, and while Greek civilization lost some of its unique beauty and originality it lived on in new forms at home as well as on foreign soil among foreign people. It is equally mistaken to speak of the period as that of Greek decadence or to treat Hellenistic history as a mere accompaniment to the simultaneous rise of Rome. It was a new creative period in the history of the human mind, in which Greeks and non-Greeks played their essential though very different parts. It even created a simplified Greek *koinē* ('common speech') and a common state of mind whereby a Greek was now a man of Greek education and no longer simply of Greek origin. Greek civilization not only conquered the Near East but influenced, however superficially, countries as far apart as Parthia and India on the one hand and Carthage and Rome on the other. There was a far-reaching fusion between Hellenistic civilization and the East; Judaism among others was partly influenced by Greek culture, and the latter had a decisive share in the formation of early Christianity.

It will be useful to distinguish various periods within the Hellenistic Age, although a clear-cut separation would be mistaken and strict adherence to the dates and meanings put forward might produce a false historical picture. However, the age may be said to fall into the following three main periods: (1) 323–280 B.C., witnessing the disintegration of Alexander's empire and the establishment of a new society of states; (2) 280–c. 160 B.C., the creative phase, characterized by balance of power, the progress of Greek culture and the Greek way of life over an ever-widening area, and the supremacy of philosophy and science; (3) c. 160–30 B.C., a period of decline under the influence, spiritual and material, of the East and Rome and of political self-destruction, a period in which irrationalism and religion prevailed.

The Hellenistic Age

Our sources vary considerably with regard to different periods, both in quantity and quality. They are fairly ample for the wars of the Diadochi (successors of Alexander). Accounts by Diodorus, Plutarch, Arrian and others survive, mainly deriving from the reliable Hieronymus of Cardia. The course of events during the following decades is obscure. Dates throughout are uncertain and often guesswork. The original historians are lost and were anyhow mostly gossipy and biased writers. For the West alone, the work of the Sicilian Timaeus provided a solid basis for later historians. From 221 B.C. onward (till 145 B.C.) there is Polybius. The many missing parts of his work are partly covered by Livy. Most of the later writers largely depend on Polybius. Poseidonius' continuation is lost, and the most important historian for the later period is Appian (second century A.D.). Later sources from Polybius onward are or were mainly centred on the relations between Rome and the Hellenistic world. For Hellenistic Judaea I and II Maccabees are essential. Scattered facts of political history throughout are mentioned by many writers. Non-literary sources (inscriptions, papyri, coins) provide useful evidence, chiefly of constitutional, administrative and economic facts, also of religion and superstition. The papyri tell a very great deal about social and economic life in Hellenistic Egypt; for many aspects they are the only source, from which it would be dangerous to generalize. It remains to say that most literary sources show the influence of some kind of propaganda; it is often difficult to paint an impartial picture of events.

2. OUTLINES OF POLITICAL HISTORY

Alexander's empire, reaching from Macedonia to the Punjab, became after his death in 323 the scene of a long struggle among his marshals, some of whom, in accordance with the wishes of the rank and file in the Macedonian army, tried to preserve the unity of the empire, as first represented by 'the kings', Alexander's illegitimate brother Philip III Arrhidaeus, a half-wit, and his posthumous infant son by Roxana, Alexander IV. Most of the generals installed by Alexander as satraps aimed however at breaking up the empire and creating realms of their own. The struggles of the 'Successors'

(Diadochi) can be divided into several phases. The central government was first represented by Antipater, viceroy in Europe; Perdiccas, viceroy of Asia and commander-in-chief; and Craterus, guardian of the kings. The chief satraps were Ptolemy in Egypt, Lysimachus in Thrace and Antigonus Monophthalmus in Phrygia; Eumenes, the only Greek among the successors, was installed in Cappadocia. A revolt in Greece, the Lamian War (323–322), was crushed by Antipater, and a revolt of Greek colonists in Bactria ended in massacre. The stealthy removal of Alexander's body to Egypt led to a war in which Perdiccas and Craterus perished. By the agreement of Triparadisus (321) Antipater was made sole viceroy, Antigonus commander in Asia and Seleucus satrap of Babylon; the kings were sent to Macedonia. This ended the first phase of the struggle (323–321).

In the second phase (321–316) the central government was decisively weakened, especially after Antipater's death (319); his successor, Polyperchon, had little authority. He and Eumenes were now the champions of unity, but the coalition of satraps, joined by Antipater's ruthless son Cassander, was too strong. While first Polyperchon and later Antigonus and Ptolemy tried to win the Greeks by proclaiming their freedom, Greece was in Cassander's hands and the philosopher Demetrius of Phaleron ruled Athens for him (317–307). The Macedonian royal house was eventually to meet a catastrophic end; Roxana and her son survived till 310 when they too fell victims to Cassander. Eumenes was defeated and executed by Antigonus (316).

In the following third phase (316–311) the aim of keeping the unity of the empire was taken over by Antigonus, but now in order to make himself supreme ruler. Supported by his brilliant son Demetrius Poliorcetes and to some extent by Polyperchon, but opposed by a strong coalition of satraps, he could not maintain his position. Demetrius was heavily beaten by Ptolemy at Gaza (312); Seleucus, previously expelled by Antigonus, regained Babylon, and in 311 a provisional truce gave all combatants a respite.

The next (fourth) phase saw Demetrius in Athens, which he liberated from Cassander's garrison (307). Ptolemy held Cyprus, the Aegean and Cyrene, but was defeated by Demetrius in a naval

The Hellenistic Age

battle off Cyprus in 306. The latter's attempt to conquer Rhodes in a famous siege (305–304) was in the end unsuccessful, and since the satraps became kings (306/305) all unification of the empire had become impossible. Demetrius had some success in Greece, but at Ipsus Lysimachus and Seleucus finally defeated Antigonus, who fell in battle (301); four powers then emerged under Lysimachus, Ptolemy, Cassander and Seleucus.

Even that was not for long. In the fifth and last phase (301–280) Demetrius, who ruled the sea, regained Greece and after Cassander's death Macedonia (294). The coalition against him was joined by Pyrrhus, king of Epirus, who also aimed at the Macedonian throne. Demetrius threw all his gains away in a disastrous campaign in Asia and ended as Seleucus' prisoner, while his son Antigonus Gonatas maintained a precarious position in Greece. New rivalries and new coalitions followed. Lysimachus' strong empire included Macedonia and most of Asia Minor; but his third marriage to Arsinoë, Ptolemy's ambitious daughter, led to the execution of his own son, who soon was avenged by Seleucus; Lysimachus fell in battle (281). Shortly afterward Seleucus was murdered by Ptolemy Ceraunus, half-brother and afterward husband of Arsinoë. For a time king of Macedonia, Ptolemy Ceraunus was killed fighting the invasion of the Celts (279), who were later defeated by the new king of Macedonia, Antigonus II Gonatas, and in Asia by Seleucus' successor, Antiochus I. Arsinoë became queen of Egypt, where her brother Ptolemy II Philadelphus had been sole ruler since 283. Under the second generation of kings the three dynasties of the Ptolemies, Seleucids and Antigonids were established. Further smaller kingdoms existed, especially in Asia Minor, where the Attalids of Pergamum began their career as an important power.

For forty years Macedonian marshals, men of unbridled passions, ambitions and energy, had battled against the survival of Alexander's empire and for the creation of new states. In these decades the foundations were laid of a new type of ruler and state and a new civilization. The three leading realms maintained a balance of power. Wars and foreign policy were essentially a constant probing of that balance and concentrated mainly on the border areas of Syria, Asia Minor and the Aegean.

During the years of struggle in the East and the emergence of monarchical rule a similar development took place in Sicily. The attempt of Timoleon (died c. 336) at restoring the autonomy of Syracuse and other city-states had only led to increased anarchy. Out of it Agathocles, who came from the ranks as a soldier, usurped power and, fighting against Carthage, soon turned the position of a city tyrant into that of the ruler of the larger part of Sicily. Despite setbacks he made himself king (305/304), as an equal to the Eastern kings. He even ruled the seas round Italy, but was unable to secure the succession; he died in 289. Pyrrhus (319–272), who had married one of his daughters, tried in vain to win the realm for his son; he was equally unsuccessful in expanding his power in Italy against Rome. It was eventually only through Roman intervention that in Syracuse a new leader, Hieron II, succeeded in establishing a kingdom after the Hellenistic fashion; after his death (216/215) it soon became part of the new Roman province of Sicily. The rivalry of Rome and Carthage prevented any balance of power in the West.

Among the rulers of the third century Ptolemy II Philadelphus (283–246) and Ptolemy III Euergetes (246–221) were the richest and the most powerful. Their aggressive policy led to three Syrian wars and to the extension of Ptolemaic influence into the Aegean world. Egyptian money brought about the Chremonidean War (267 or 266–262) in which many Greek states fought against Macedonia; it ended in Antigonus' victory. He was now the absolute master of Greece, and Athens never regained political importance. The Ptolemies conquered parts of Asia Minor and created a protectorate over a league of the islanders, but later lost all Aegean positions, temporarily even the African dominion of Cyrene. Macedonia obtained maritime supremacy in the battles of Cos and Andros (the dates are uncertain). Syria and Palestine, not least because of their importance for trade, remained disputed countries between Seleucids and Ptolemies.

The Seleucid empire, on the other hand, had troubles of its own. Extending over most of Alexander's Asiatic empire, it could not be kept together. The Indian satrapies gained independence, and Asoka founded (c. 275) a large Buddhist empire which remained open to

Greek cultural influence. Around 250 Bactria became independent under Greek rulers. Farther west a national Iranian movement led to the foundation of the Parthian kingdom of the Arsacids, and Armenia was later lost to a local dynast. Thus the Seleucid empire was thrown back on its central and western parts. There were also troubles inside the Seleucid family and with the Ptolemies, which led to the Third Syrian War (246–241) when Ptolemy Euergetes marched beyond the Euphrates; but he soon lost most of his conquests. New dynastic strife among the sons of Antiochus II caused the loss of Asia Minor to the Galatians (a splinter group of the great Celtic invasion of 279) until Attalus I, the ruler of Pergamum, defeated them c. 230 and became king of an independent state. The Seleucids had lost their Aegean seaboard.

In Greece the third century saw the rise to power of the Aetolian and Achaean leagues. The former, holding Delphi and dominating central Greece, extended their power by land and by sea. This was the only state in Greece always free from Macedonia; of formidable strength, it was lacking in constructive statesmanship. It was different with the Achaean league under the leadership of Aratus who for almost thirty years was general every other year. In fighting Macedonia and the various tyrants (usually pro-Macedonian) he eventually succeeded by a surprise attack in capturing Corinth, the Macedonian key stronghold. Later the two leagues, though beginning to become rivals, were able to extend their power and further to weaken the position of Macedonia. The Achaean league included the whole Peloponnese except Sparta and Elis, while the Aetolians, by extending their federal citizenship, held central and northern Greece from sea to sea. Antigonus III Doson (229–221) restored peace and royal power in Macedonia but left the leagues alone. The time of the really great kings had passed, though Antiochus III and Philip V were still to show remarkable ability and power. Of the city-states none was important; Athens, the acknowledged cultural centre of Greece, had gained a kind of *de facto* neutrality. Only Sparta still played a part of its own. After Agis IV had tried and failed, Cleomenes III succeeded in carrying through a social revolution (227). Cleomenes, driven by personal ambition, then went to war with the Achaean league. He found allies in Egypt and the Aetolian league. Aratus, between two hostile powers and afraid of social revolts, asked his old enemy Macedonia for help. Antigonus Doson received Corinth back and re-established the Hellenic league. Cleomenes, defeated at Sellasia (222), perished in Egypt. Antigonus Doson entered Sparta, the first enemy to do so, and Sparta became a member of the Achaean league; its political role was finished, in spite of a short aftermath under Nabis (207–192).

A new period began with the accession in 223 to the Seleucid throne of Antiochus III (known as 'the Great') and in 221 of Philip V to that of Macedonia. It is the epoch when Polybius' *History* opens; it is also the moment when 'the clouds from the West' began to threaten the Hellenistic world and its balance of power. Rome, by defeating the Illyrian pirates, ruled the Adriatic sea and became Macedonia's neighbour. The young Philip V, facing a Greece disrupted by war and devastation, accepted in 217 the peace of Naupactus, the last Greek peace before Roman interference. Then he became involved in the Second Punic War in 215, though he was unable to support Hannibal against Rome. In this First Macedonian War the Aetolians allied with Rome while the Achaean league, reformed by Philopoimen, supported Macedonia. The war ended in the inconclusive peace of Phoenice (205). Meanwhile Antiochus III succeeded in restoring his almost disrupted empire, though he lost against Ptolemy IV the battle of Raphia (217), in which native Egyptian troops for the first time played an important part. It was a decisive event for the growing Egyptian nationalism and thus indicated the decline of Ptolemaic rule while, rather surprisingly, the Seleucid empire was once again consolidated. Antiochus, having secured most of the western half of his empire, campaigned for eight years (212–205) in the East and forced the kings there to accept Seleucid supremacy. These vassals naturally remained loyal only as long as the central government was strong.

In 205 Ptolemy V, a child, succeeded to the throne of Egypt. Antiochus and Philip immediately attacked the Ptolemaic dominions. By his harsh methods of warfare Philip alienated the Greeks, and in 200, when the Romans had their hands free, the Egyptians, Rhodians and Attalus I of Pergamum urged them to intervene.

Hence started Roman expansion to the east, and the balance of power among the Hellenistic states was soon to be destroyed.

The Second Macedonian War (200–197) resulted in Philip's defeat at Cynoscephalae; by the peace terms he lost his fleet and his possessions outside Macedonia, was obliged to give hostages and pay an indemnity, and became Rome's ally. The Roman general, the philhellene T. Quintus Flaminius, solemnly declared all Greeks free (196). This was received with enthusiasm, and though it soon led to disillusionment, it was first a great help for Rome in its dealings with Antiochus, who, having reduced Pergamum, had crossed into Thrace (196). Roman protests were disregarded. The Romans evacuated Greece in 194, but Roman 'advice' remained the decisive factor in the internal Greek struggles. In 192 the Aetolian league, dissatisfied with Roman settlement, invited Antiochus to Greece, but the promised Greek revolt did not materialize, and Philip and the Achaean league actually supported the Romans. Defeated at Thermopylae (191), Antiochus returned to Asia; supported by the fleets of Pergamum and Rhodes, the Romans repeatedly defeated his fleet and crossed into Asia Minor to defeat him on land at Magnesia (winter 190/189). The Aetolians surrendered to M. Fulvius Nobilior (189), becoming subordinate allies of Rome, and in 188 the peace of Apamea was ratified, by which Antiochus lost all his possessions in Asia Minor except Cilicia. Most of these passed to Eumenes II of Pergamum; the Rhodians also profited by the peace and ruled the seas. Many of the Greek cities of Asia Minor were declared free, though others became subject to Pergamum. Next year (187) Antiochus was killed in a local fight. The Seleucid empire was still a great power, but practically confined to Mesopotamia and Syria, with a weak hold on the seven 'upper provinces' in the east.

In Greece the forcible annexation of Sparta by the Achaean league under Philopoimen (188) provoked repeated Roman intervention, and relations between Rome and the league worsened. Philip's consolidation of his remaining kingdom made him suspect at Rome. After his death (179) his less-gifted son Perseus continued his policy. Further complaints by Eumenes led to the Third Macedonian War (171–168); three years of indecisive warfare ended in the victory of L. Aemilius Paullus at Pydna. Macedonia was divided into four independent republics. Greece was treated severely; the Aetolian league was dissolved; the Achaean league, although it had offered support to Rome, was forced to surrender 1,000 hostages (including Polybius). The Rhodians' offer of mediation cost them their gains by the peace of Apamea, and Delos soon replaced Rhodes as the commercial centre of the Aegean; even Eumenes fell into disfavour, a fact which strengthened his position among the Asiatic Greeks and the Galatians.

In 149 a pretender, Andriscus, gained considerable support in Macedonia but was defeated by Q. Caecilius Metellus the following year. Macedonia, with Illyria and Epirus, became a Roman province. Achaean operations against Sparta led to war with Rome (146): L. Mummius defeated the league and sacked Corinth. Greece was placed under the supervision of the governor of Macedonia (until 27 B.C., when it became the province of Achaea).

The pro-Roman policy maintained by Pergamum under Eumenes II (king 197–159) was continued by his brother Attalus II (159–138), who had not shared his disfavour after 168; under him the realm flourished and prospered. The expansion of Bithynia under Prusias I (king c. 230–182) and II (182–149) menaced Pergamene territory, but the Romans intervened in Attalus' favour (159). The last Attalid, Attalus III (138–133), while giving freedom to the city of Pergamum, bequeathed his kingdom and his treasures to Rome. A pretender, Aristonicus, fired by Stoic ('socialist') ideas, led a serious revolt (132–129) in Asia Minor, but in 129 Manius Aquilius was able to organize the Roman province of Asia which covered the larger part of the Pergamene empire.

In Asia itself, after the quiet reign of Seleucus IV (187–175), his brother Antiochus IV Epiphanes pursued a more active policy. An Egyptian attack on Palestine (170) was countered by an invasion of Egypt, in which Antiochus captured the young king Ptolemy VI Philometor, whereupon the Alexandrians proclaimed as king his younger brother, Ptolemy VIII Euergetes. Antiochus' second invasion (168) ended in his humiliating withdrawal on the orders of the Roman envoy Gaius Popilius Laenas, leaving the two Ptolemies as joint kings of Egypt, with their sister Cleopatra II as queen of Ptolemy VI. Inside his kingdom Antiochus promoted Hellenism and in pursuance of this policy rededicated the Temple at Jerusalem to Olympian Zeus (168); this provoked great hostility and finally the Maccabean revolt of the Jews (167–142). On his way to tackle the growing power of the Parthians in the east, Antiochus died (163); the dynastic struggles following his death led to the disintegration of the Seleucid empire. The last Seleucid to unite Syria, Palestine and Mesopotamia was Antiochus VII Sidetes (139–129): after his death in battle against the Parthians, the children of Cleopatra Thea (daughter of Ptolemy VI) by him and his brother Demetrius II (king 145–139) and 129–126/125) formed rival branches and continued to dispute a rapidly declining kingdom.

From the beginning of the third century the kingdom of Pontus on the southern coast of the Black Sea had been growing, although the murder of Mithradates V (c. 121) led to the loss of Phrygia (joined to Asia c. 116) and Paphlagonia. The attempts of Mithradates VI Eupator to extend his rule in Asia Minor led to conflict with Nicomedes III of Bithynia and Roman intervention (c. 95 and 92). The First Mithradatic War (88–85) began with a massacre of Italians in Asia. Most of the Greeks in Asia and many in Europe, feeling deep hatred for the Romans, supported Mithradates, but the victories in Greece of L. Cornelius Sulla, who sacked Athens (86), and in Asia of Gaius Flavius Fimbria, obliged him to accept the peace of Dardanus, which was comparatively lenient. Greece, however, suffered badly and never – not even under Augustus – fully recovered. The Second Mithradatic War (83–82) was unimportant, but in 74 Nicomedes IV's bequest of Bithynia to the Romans led to the Third Mithradatic War (74–63), in the course of which Mithradates and his son-in-law Tigranes of Armenia were defeated by the Roman general L. Licinius Lucullus, and Tigranes forced (69) to evacuate Syria, which he had occupied in 83. In 64 Gnaeus Pompeius Magnus (Pompey) disregarded the last Seleucid claimants and annexed Syria as a Roman province: Bithynia with western Pontus also became a province (63), and client-kings were recognized in Armenia, Commagene, Cappadocia and elsewhere. Although the Romans exploited the peoples of their empire, they saved the East from complete chaos and Hellenistic civilization from destruction.

In Egypt, the joint rule of Ptolemy VI and VIII was not a success; Roman arbitration gave Ptolemy VIII Cyrene as a separate kingdom (163). Ptolemy VI's support of successive Seleucid pretenders brought about his death near Antioch (145); Ptolemy VIII killed his nephew Ptolemy VII, married Cleopatra and became king of the whole realm, but failed to establish a strong national monarchy, partly because of the existence of two queens, Cleopatra II and her daughter Cleopatra III; anarchy was widespread. At Ptolemy's death (116) Cyrene passed to the illegitimate Ptolemy Apion, who bequeathed it to Rome (96), Egypt and Cyprus to Cleopatra III and her sons Ptolemy IX Soter and Ptolemy X Alexander. Although domestic strife continued until Ptolemy IX became sole ruler (88), the kingdom did not disintegrate entirely, but Palestine was finally lost. Egypt, even under bad government, remained a very rich country. In 80 one illegitimate son of Ptolemy IX, Ptolemy XII Auletes (80–58 and 55–51), became king of Egypt, and another son became king of Cyprus (annexed by Rome in 58). Auletes saved his throne by bribing Roman senators; on his death his son Ptolemy XIII and daughter Cleopatra VII became joint rulers. During Julius Caesar's visit to Egypt (48–47) the boy-king Ptolemy XIII was killed in battle against him; Cleopatra was then associated with her younger brother Ptolemy XIV and after his death (44) with her son Ptolemy XV, nicknamed Caesarion and said to be Caesar's son. She, the most famous of all Hellenistic rulers, was able even to frighten Rome. After the defeat and death of Antony and Cleopatra, Egypt became a province of the Roman empire (30).

3. THE HELLENISTIC STATES

There was no single type of Hellenistic state. The Greek city-state (polis) survived. Athens remained a cultural centre, Sparta went through an inner revolution to become a museum of its own past, old trading centres like Corinth or new ones like Rhodes and Delos flourished at times. A well-preserved example of a small prosperous Hellenistic town in Asia Minor is Priene near Miletus. Many new city-states were created by the new rulers. They all had their officials, councils and assemblies but frequently the polis constitution was little more than a façade. In fact, the city-state was no longer a power adequate to the changed conditions of the age, and in most cases it was included in a larger realm.

Attempts by the Greeks themselves to overcome the weakness of the single polis were made by the creation of unions and federations. Polis autonomy could be subject to a federal body on a tribal or regional basis. Its ultimate form as a true federal state with double citizenship and strong federal authority was achieved, above all, in the Aetolian and Achaean leagues, the two most powerful states of Hellenistic Greece. Their constitutions were adaptations of polis constitutions with a primary assembly, a council and annual officials. The council was composed of representatives of the member states; it is the first clear example of the representative system in Greece. These leagues were territorial states and the citizens of the member states were citizens of the federal state. Simply on account of distances, the assembly rarely met and even the council did not sit permanently. The officials therefore, whether a small board or a military leader (*strategus*), were more powerful than normal polis officials, and the leagues were regarded by the kings as powers on almost equal level with their own realms.

Sometimes a league was founded and controlled by one of the rulers, e.g. the islanders' league by the Ptolemies. The League of Corinth, on the other hand, founded by Philip II in 337 and renewed by Antigonus I and again by Antigonus III Doson, retained the character of the earlier Greek form of a federation under a leading power (*hegemon*), in this case the Macedonian king. Monarchy had entered Greek political life even earlier. After the end, in the fifth century, of rule by tyrants in the city-states, the monarchical idea had gained influence again in the fourth century, both in actual politics and in theory. Yet it was not till Alexander that monarchy became the most important factor in Greek political structure. Whatever the differences in the size and character of the states, the territorial monarchy was the essential Hellenistic type of state. Created by Macedonian generals and culminating in the establishment of three large realms, the type was repeated all over Asia in smaller powers which were ruled by Greeks or hellenized Orientals. A territorial monarchy could even develop from a city-state as in

Syracuse and Pergamum, and the external appearance of Hellenistic kingship was sometimes imitated by polis rulers such as Areus
and Nabis in Sparta. Of most of the monarchies so little is known
that the picture must be drawn mainly from the three great powers
and Pergamum.

Only in Macedonia was the king a national leader acclaimed by
the army; in Asia and Egypt the kings were foreign rulers who had
come as conquerors and established an absolute monarchy over
Greeks and non-Greeks. Gradually the Macedonian monarchy too
grew much more absolute. The land generally belonged to the
king – not in Macedonia or in the city-states, but in the Macedonian dominions just as in Egypt or Pergamum; even in the
Seleucid empire private ownership of land was largely due to royal
gifts. The Macedonians were the ruling people of the world, but
outside Macedonia they were a small minority who upheld Macedonian traditions, though even in Macedonia they accepted Greek
culture. Soon it was hardly possible to draw a clear line between
Macedonians and Greeks; the numbers of the latter were large in
each of the realms. They had mostly emigrated from their poor
and overpopulated country, and, serving as officers, officials or military colonists, or working as scholars, artists or engineers, became
the chief support of the new rulers. The close proximity of Greeks
and Orientals led to much intermixture of blood and civilization.
Everybody was subject to the king, and citizenship had become a
purely local affair in the city-states. Most of the native peasants,
though in general not deliberately oppressed, remained poor and
sometimes exploited and misused. In the long run however their
innate nationalism, helped by their large numbers, challenged
Greek domination and even Greek language and culture. From the
end of the third century the Greeks were in retreat. In the cities,
however, Greeks and hellenized Orientals, using the gymnasium as
their centre, for a long time maintained their way of life and their
social status.

Alexander had tried – not entirely successfully – to combine his
Macedonian kingship with the position of Egyptian Pharaohs and
Persian kings; that is to say, a people's monarchy with theocratic
despotism. His successors, within narrower aims, followed his

example and created the ultimate form of Hellenistic monarchy. The consent of the army assembly became a mere formality, even in Macedonia. The king ruled without legal limitation to his power, though he could delegate it to high officials. Land and people, with certain exceptions, were his property; that is why some of the kings could bequeath their states as well as their personal treasures to Rome. Court hierarchy and etiquette gradually developed, with 'friends' (*philoi*) as a permanent institution, 'kinsmen' (*syngeneis*) as specially honoured courtiers, with 'bodyguards' and 'pages' and other personal titles. Succession was in the male line and great efforts were made to strengthen the dynasty by claiming descent from respectable ancestors, usually starting from a Greek god, by securing succession through joint rule of father and son and by stressing the role played by the queen. She was the king's 'sister', whether actually as in Egypt, or only nominally. The strongest support both of monarchy and of dynasty was, apart from the army, ruler worship. It could be founded by a city-state, expressing thanks and flattery and fear, or established by the king as an official dynastic cult which usually included the queens. Ruler cult, a particular and important feature of Hellenistic kingship, followed the example of Alexander, but would not have been possible without such Greek traditions as the anthropomorphic nature of religion and myth, the heroization of dead men and the occasional worship of great men even during their lifetime. However, the geographical facts (Macedonia had practically no ruler worship) and the peculiar nature of Hellenistic ruler cult point to Oriental influence as well. Nowhere but in the East was the soil prepared in a similar degree. The Ptolemies were Egyptian gods like the Pharaohs, and the Seleucids and other Eastern dynasties followed earlier kings who ruled 'by the grace of the gods'. Ruler worship has been called a political religion; though the political side was usually the stronger one, the other must not be forgotten. It is mistaken, for instance, to explain the cult of a ruler by a polis as a legal fiction to justify the relation between polis and monarch; it is perhaps more to the point to derive them from that innate Greek feeling of the identity of the political and the religious community. At Doura-Europus, a foundation of Seleucus I, the cult of the founder was fully alive as late as

A.D. 180. A particular feature of the dynastic cult was the distinction of kings or royal couples by secondary names, some of which indicated divine character (*Soter*, 'saviour'; *Theos*, 'god'; *Epiphanes*, 'god manifest'), others (e.g. *Philopator*, 'father-loving') simply the coherence of the dynasty. The cult was intended to serve the unity of the state; the weaker the kings, the more emphatic became their divinity and the greater the number of royal names.

The kings ruled by edicts, and it was the main task of the officials to carry them out. Administration varied according to the nature of the different states or their parts, but everywhere royal officials were needed both in the central government and to administer the parts of the realm. Survivals of earlier systems, such as the Macedonian aristocracy, the dynasts and temple states in Asia, or the priests in Egypt, though all not without power, were outside the bureaucracy, while the administrative system, though inherited from earlier empires, was far more thoroughly organized, chiefly because of advanced Greek standards in law, finance and administration. Greeks filled most of the higher posts; the lower offices were left to the natives, though they later rose to the higher grades as well. The new bureaucratic system under the king reached its highest perfection in the over-centralized organization of Egypt. The most important of all officials here was the *dioecetes* who was primarily the finance minister but also the chief deputy for the king and in charge of everything except military and foreign affairs. In the administration outside the central government, the leading officials in most states were the *strategi* (originally 'generals'); they varied in competence and power, but everywhere developed from military into civil officers. In the countryside, especially in Egypt, there was a large body of civil servants, down to the heads and scribes of the villages. In the Seleucid empire the *strategi* gradually replaced the satraps; within their provinces they could even act as high priests of the ruler cult. Together with dependent kings and dynasts, the Seleucid *strategi* were a powerful instrument of decentralization. The technical perfection of administration in most states was at first very good indeed, and the king's control during the third and part of the second century usually fairly strict. The Greeks soon learned the paper work of an administration for which they originally were not trained; but from the second century onward corruption and inefficiency grew alarmingly. Weak government, the increase in the number of native officials and the tempting opportunities of bureaucratic power gradually corrupted the system.

Within the framework of the monarchical realms the Greek city-state gained special importance. Old and newly founded cities were the centres of Greek life and for that reason a vital factor in the political and social structure, although standing outside state organization. Alexander, taking up an idea propagated by Isocrates, for instance, founded new cities in the East on a large scale, and he was followed by the early Seleucids; they also founded military colonies (many called Macedonian, though probably mixed with Greeks), some of which developed into full cities. New cities could also be established by synoecism, the union of existing cities or villages. The vast majority, however, of new foundations were heirs to earlier non-Greek towns whose native upper class usually adopted the Greek way of life. Colonization and hellenization went hand in hand; frequently the city population was only partially Greek by origin. The typical polis institutions, however, political as well as social, were accepted and adapted everywhere, though city offices of an unpolitical nature, such as the gymnasiarchs and the agoranomi, gained importance, and private associations partly replaced the bonds of citizenship. The Hellenistic polis was little more than a municipal community.

A special part was played by the capital cities. The Ptolemies did not found cities in Egypt except for two of little importance, Ptolemais and Philadelphia. But Alexandria (called 'near Egypt', not 'in' it), as the capital of an empire, the royal residence and a combination of various peoples and their political bodies (*politeumata*), was no ordinary polis; its Greek section, though representative of the whole city, may not even have had a council. Other capital cities were of a similar type, but it is significant for Seleucid decentralization that there were two royal capitals, Seleucia on the Tigris and Antioch, and other provincial capitals of considerable importance such as Sardes. Pergamum, an old Greek polis, was turned into a royal capital with hardly any autonomy left.

The relationship between king and polis varied widely, and so do modern views on it, mainly because there was no single clear-cut solution for the tension between the king's supremacy and the freedom of the city-state. The kings, trying to keep their realms as coherent as possible, could not accept within their territories any real sovereignty but their own. The cities, regarding their autonomy as essential, claimed to be independent allies of the rulers, a pretence sometimes accepted by the kings. The cities in Greece and the Aegean largely maintained the appearance of autonomy and it was the policy of some of the earlier rulers to proclaim and to guarantee their freedom. This proved to be a piece of valuable propaganda. Autonomy theoretically implied the city's own laws, an independent foreign policy, right of coinage and immunity from tribute and garrison; in practice these rules were frequently broken and hardly any city could maintain independence in foreign affairs. Generally autonomy was replaced by an exchange between king and city of *eunoia*, good will on his and loyalty on the city's part. Local government was usually in the hands of partisans of the king, and a shift of power among the rulers might lead to internal changes. When a royal governor, normally the commander of a garrison, was appointed to administer the city, autonomy had practically gone. The king would convey to the city, either through the governor or directly, his demands or his favours (as, for example, the grant of the right of asylum, a treasured privilege); he could even interfere in the city's domestic affairs and jurisdiction.

It was less the outdated constitution and the claim for autonomy that counted than the fact that the cities represented Greek urban life in non-Greek surroundings, that they provided for the government's need of officers, officials and experts and that they were a training ground for unpolitical municipal self-government. City life in the monarchies strongly contrasted with the countryside, which was hardly hellenized. With the decline of the central power, this contrast became a conflict which had grave consequences.

4. SOCIAL AND ECONOMIC CONDITIONS

In this field knowledge is particularly limited and fragmentary; but obviously the differences in the political sphere were reflected in social and economic life. The chief sources of trouble were never removed. There always were tensions between city-states and monarchies, between Greeks and Orientals, between rich and poor. There was, on the other hand, a unity behind these tensions which socially and economically was due to the Greek or hellenized city population in East and West. Whatever its political position, the polis was the centre of economic and social life, in spite of the general importance of agriculture. Town planning and building, business and trade, language and law, religion and education, entertainment and family life were substantially the same everywhere; the special conditions in Egypt were the exception. The natives however were not included, with the exception of the hellenized upper class; that is to say, the vast majority of the population remained outside Hellenistic society.

The social structure chiefly depended on the 'Greek dispersion', the emigration of many thousands of Greeks and far fewer Macedonians from Greece and the Aegean, and the part they played in the new monarchies. A small minority filled the higher ranks of officialdom, of army and navy and of the court; they were in general very well off. Large numbers, on the other hand, served as soldiers and settlers or were merchants and craftsmen, teachers and doctors, artists and engineers. They were Greeks or hellenized Macedonians, increasingly mixed with hellenized Orientals. It was they who represented a kind of middle class, united by their education, their moderate wealth, their private associations and their language. Education was essential. A man was a Greek when he had gone to school (mostly private, sometimes endowed by rich patrons or kings), had taken part in the physical and intellectual training of the *ephebi* (no longer a military service), and belonged to a group based on a gymnasium. On this basis he would be a Greek gentleman or at least a person fit to serve as an official. The financing and supervision of the educational system was in the hands of the local authorities, the polis or *politeuma*. Whatever native aristocracy or middle class existed would gradually be drawn into the city society. Greek exclusiveness relaxed more and more and some of the un-educated Greeks must have gone down to the lower classes. The way of life of the upper classes was similar to that of the corresponding classes in the motherland, the upper-class citizens and the prosperous metics (resident non-citizens), who since pre-Hellenistic times had had about the same social standing. Everywhere social and economic life was upheld by the activities of a *bourgeoisie*.

Naturally they could not have had their professional as well as their prosperous life without the labouring class, which in the East was practically identical with the native population (whether freemen, serfs or slaves) while in Greece and the Aegean it was represented by declining numbers of poor free peasants and workers and a large slave population. In East and West the lower classes, especially during the second century B.C., were always on the verge of revolting and often did revolt. But a distinction must be made between the conditions in the old Greek cities and the new monarchies.

The part played by the Greeks generally made the citizen *bourgeoisie* in the old country more conscious of the common bonds between all Greeks. *Homonoia* ('concord') became a favourite slogan, though that only shows that polis individualism was still strong. For instance each city still had its own calendar; on the other hand it was common practice to engage judges from other cities. The prosperity of the third century led to increased trading and travelling and to a widening of the horizons. Philosophy, especially Stoicism, helped to undermine the old mentality and to create an atmosphere in which the equality of men seemed no longer an entirely Utopian ideal. Yet the *bourgeoisie*, composed mainly of wealthy landowners, of men who owned ships or workshops and of capitalists who employed slaves or hired them out, still clung to the traditions of polis life, in particular to those of religion. In general, they led an easy life of leisure and culture. The conflict between rich and poor persisted and towards the end of the third century the social and economic problems of a depopulated country became so pressing that the usual neglect was no longer possible. The *bourgeoisie* itself, apart from a few very rich, felt

the decline in purchasing power of the masses for whom they provided as local producers and traders. Emigration had stopped,
families were severely restricted by infanticide, interest on money
rose, wages remained low, grain was often in short supply and
famines were fairly frequent. It was only natural that the lower
classes began to revolt against the ruling oligarchies. Best known is
the revolution in Sparta, led by two of the kings themselves (Agis
IV and Cleomenes III) and directed against the small class of rich
landowners. Here as elsewhere the chief demands were cancella-
tion of debts and redistribution of land. Another example is the
revolt of Aristonicus in Asia Minor. These revolts threatened the very
life of the upper classes, and resistance to them was supported first
by Macedonia and later by Rome. That meant that the revolts never
succeeded.

Some of the Aegean cities on the other hand, geographically and
politically on the fringe of the Hellenistic world, retained their
prosperity as important centres for most of the international trade.
The same seems true of some of the cities in Asia Minor, and the
bourgeoisie there must largely have kept its original character. In the
monarchies in general, however, it was a class of trained professionals. The creation of the Greek bureaucracy, however much it
owed to its Oriental predecessors, was an astonishing achievement.
Philosophical treatises were of little help; the success was largely
due to hard work and quickly gained experience on the part of the
kings and their high officials. It was similar with army and navy,
though these were largely Greek in their lower ranks as well. In this
field, technical handbooks written by experts (e.g. on siege machines and fortifications) were important. The writers and scholars
of Alexandria and Pergamum were in a sense also professionals;
on the fringe of this upper class of professionals were entertainers
like the Dionysiac *technitae* (travelling religious companies of
theatrical performers) and the teachers and physicians, many of
whom were employed by city or state.

Generally in the cities where economic life suffered comparatively
little from royal interference, free enterprise in manufacture and
trade played an important part; in the monarchies economic
organization by the state was decisive. The kings needed large sums

to maintain political power and military efficiency. Both civil service and armed forces were very costly. The armies had become larger, and though the kings to some extent used conscription they had to pay for large numbers of mercenaries and the expensive technical equipment of army and navy. State finance and general economy were therefore closely tied together. The king was the state. The king's economic power made of Egypt an enormous household and royal business; other states, though far from showing the same consistency, yet displayed similar trends. A primary reason for the new economic atmosphere of the Hellenistic world was the abundance of money after Alexander had put the Persian treasures into circulation, an additional reason for the fact that up to c. 150 B.C. large amounts of capital, assembled in the countries around the eastern Mediterranean, were used for fostering trade and business farther east. The economic prosperity of the first half of the third century was followed by a slow decline which after 200 B.C. led to a dangerous impoverishment of Greece and to inflation in Egypt, while the intervention of Rome particularly affected Macedonia and Asia. There were still periods of prosperity, especially in Asia Minor, but on the whole economic standards were reduced.

Agriculture remained the basis of economic life. New land (obtained for instance by draining swamps like the Fayûm in Egypt), some small improvements in cultivation, intensification of vine growing, introduction of foreign plants and of a few domestic animals were some of the features of Hellenistic agriculture. There was a growing number of large estates, and Greek experience joined hands with the greater possibilities that the East granted in land extension and manpower. The estate of the *dioecetes* Apollonius, known from papyri found in the Fayûm, is the outstanding but not the only example. The king, however, was the greatest landowner. The royal domains were very extensive; arable land and pastures were worked by the king's peasants (in Egypt native tenants who paid rent, otherwise generally native serfs); quarries, mines, forests were exploited on his behalf, partly by slaves. All land not directly owned by the king was liable to heavy taxation (often a tenth). In Egypt, the land given to temples, high officials or settlers (cleruchs) was held as a temporary royal gift, not as a property; a negligible part was private land.

In manufacture small workshops were still the rule; there was no industrialization and little mass production. The king, by taxation and monopolies, had the main share in the profits. Salt was generally an object of royal monopoly and among the Egyptian monopolies those of oil, papyrus and grain were prominent. Production and sale were closely connected, and trade partly in official hands, partly subject to high custom duties covering import and export as well as transit trade. There was some room for private enterprise, but the harbours as well as the caravan routes were officially controlled and protected; brigandage and piracy were largely suppressed. Commerce was generally helped by the unification of coinage. Only two standards existed: the Attic, which since Alexander had been adopted by Macedonia and the Asian states; and the Phoenician, used by the Ptolemies. Trade was probably the one part of economic life that had changed most clearly, compared with Classical times; its geographical extension was matched by technical improvements.

The most elaborate and best-known system of state economy is that of the Ptolemies, and the apparatus needed for tax assessment and collection, for controlling the officials and for exploiting country and people without destroying their ability to provide grain and money, was enormous. It was a system based on strict organization and compulsion and it made the Ptolemies the richest rulers in the world. The ordinary peasants however remained poor and the general standard of living low. Foreign trade was to a large extent in luxury goods and slaves, and, though in times of strong government and economic prosperity conditions were satisfactory for a fairly large section of the population, these conditions never lasted long and never reached the lowest level of the people. Oriental fatalism helped to keep things going, but when the Greeks too began to suffer the decline became general. It was saved from its ultimate consequences by Roman intervention, but in that case the cure was probably worse than the disease.

5. HELLENISTIC CIVILIZATION

'Civilization' is a vague expression, but it would be fair to assume that it implied the standards of life, thought and art of the educated class, in which the lower classes had some share. The unity and essential uniformity of Hellenistic civilization is beyond doubt. It was the civilization of those who spoke the common Greek language (*koinē*), a simplified version of the Attic dialect, enriched by new words. If the upper classes almost everywhere, and part of the lower classes as well, were hellenized, that above all meant the use of the Greek language. Without this universal language there would never have been a universal civilization nor a universal religion. Native languages usually were kept alive locally, and the Semitic East even developed a kind of non-Greek *koinē*, Aramaic. Jesus spoke Aramaic, but the Gospels were written in Greek.

As mentioned above, the second and the third part of the whole period must be distinguished. In the former phase rationalism, realism and science prevailed over the forces of irrationalism, religion and superstition, which gained supremacy in the later phase. Such divisions naturally provide only a rough picture and are far too sweeping, but they may help to sort out the main tendencies of the age. Euhemerus (c. 300) can be taken as typical of the first phase of the Hellenistic Age: he wrote a fantastic travel story to show that the gods were in reality great men of the distant past. This theory may be regarded as a rationalist version of the old Greek feeling that there was no unbridgeable gulf between god and man; it continued at the same time the rationalist explanation of myth of the fifth century. Even so Euhemerus went further and reflected significant trends of his own times. In the long run, however, he could not satisfy any spiritual needs.

The earlier period was in many respects a continuation of the Classical Age. It is easy to find forerunners in the fourth century; e.g. in the methods of higher education, either philosophical as practised by Plato, or rhetorical as practised by Isocrates. Athens remained the home of philosophy. Rhetoric was in fact the predominant element of Hellenistic education. This was so although its principal use in Classical times, in politics and the law courts, had lost its importance. It might still happen that orators (or indeed philosophers) were chosen to act as ambassadors, but even then the aim of oratory was less persuasion than to make an impression by a set speech of what the Greeks called the epideictic ('showpiece') kind. To deliver public lectures was the chief activity of a finished orator, apart from teaching rhetoric. The part played by rhetoric in education can hardly be overestimated. The original idea was that good speaking derived from good thinking; but the complex schemes of rhetorical instruction lost sight of that and produced a technical formalism no longer connected with reality. It had a strong and on the whole pernicious influence on every branch of literature, although it certainly contributed to the unity of Hellenistic civilization. Leading to monotony and emptiness or to the artificial and inflated style of the 'Asianic' school, it yet must not be regarded as void of educational and cultural values. Even in the last century B.C. there was a school of sound rhetoric in Rhodes which exercised a strong influence on Cicero.

One other legacy of Classical Athens should be mentioned, the New Comedy of Menander and others. Works of high literary art, the comedies with their conventional situations and stock characters (though these were admirably depicted as individuals) reflect the spirit rather than the actual life of the *bourgeoisie* of the decade after Alexander's death. The real life of that class was still predominantly civic; there is no sign of this in New Comedy; reality could not consist of those always repeated plots built round seduced girls, cunning slaves, cruel fathers, boastful soldiers and the rest. The comedies, following Euripides rather than Aristophanes, displayed a tame eroticism and, like Theophrastus' *Characters*, an intense interest in unusual individuals and human emotions. The same interest is evident in the realism of Hellenistic art, its portraits as well as its genre scenes. While there is no clear influence of philosophy or rhetoric in New Comedy, its authors shared the widespread belief in the rule of Fate (Tyche).

The high esteem of rhetoric is one sign among many of the technical character of the age – 'technical' not in the modern sense but in the Greek meaning of expert handling, usually based on the knowledge of fixed rules. In literature, learning and playful versatility became more important than creative enthusiasm, experimenting with language and metre or good taste more important than a serious relationship to myth and religion. Literature and literary scholarship developed side by side and influenced one another. For example, Demetrius of Phaleron, pupil of Theophrastus and for ten years the philosophical and aristocratic ruler of Athens, went to Egypt and advised Ptolemy I when he founded the Museum (not a museum in the modern sense but rather a research institute) at Alexandria. This, with its large library, became the meeting place of scholars and writers; from there, ultimately, and not from Plato's Academy, derive modern libraries, universities and academies. Callimachus, who was a leading poet of the third century, was also responsible for the catalogue of the library. The works of few writers have survived, and what we know is only a small part of a very large production. Writers of all kinds were in demand. There was not only royal patronage but also an increased reading public, including female readers. The papyri that have survived reflect the enormous number of books on all levels, Classical as well as contemporary; the papyrus trade must have been largely book trade. Alexandria was the chief centre, but substantial libraries existed at other places as well.

The combination of literature and scholarship, intensified by the seclusion in which the men at the Museum lived, hardly made for great poetry. There were also petty quarrels between the poets, though that may be taken as the birth pangs of a new type of man of letters. With all their learnedness and artificiality the Alexandrian poets maintained a remarkable poetic level (they also greatly influenced the Latin poets, particularly Catullus and Virgil). Newly discovered papyri have heightened the reputation of Callimachus. Theocritus, famous as the originator of pastoral poetry, was perhaps an even better poet when, as in his *Mimes* and sometimes in his *Idylls*, he turned to genuine popular material. Apollonius of Rhodes in his *Argonautica* made an imaginative attempt to renew the Homeric tradition, while Aratus of Soli in his didactic poem on the stars, *Phaenomena*, wrote in the tradition of Hesiod; the book was also intended for practical use by sailors, being based on a fourth-century prose treatise by Eudoxus. Callimachus and other poets wrote hymns, *epyllia* (a kind of mythological short story in verse), and epigrams. The last have been called the characteristic Hellenistic form of poetry; referring no longer to heroic deeds but to the lives and deaths, love and revelry of ordinary people, they reflect the temper of the age. The epigram flourished as late as c. 100 B.C., the date of the *Garland* of Meleager of Gadara; but eventually it too was corrupted by rhetoric.

Literature had to cater for the entertainment of an increasing audience. Popular festivals and shows abounded in the Hellenistic world; but apart from the authors of New Comedy the playwrights are practically unknown. There were frequent performances of Classical drama, especially Euripides. A kind of dramatic poetry, though not meant to be staged, were the *Mimiambi* of Herodas, realistic dialogues full of satire and obscenity. It seems that the mimes and pantomimes (ballets), the most popular forms of dramatic entertainment under the Roman empire, also had their origin in the Hellenistic period. They showed what generally can be called significant features of Hellenistic literature and art: a growing display of realism and disharmony, of emotion and exaltation, of eroticism subtle or crude.

The same features, combined with the fruits of rhetoric, can be discovered in much of the prose writing. For the historians this involved a conflict, since dramatization and rhetorical writing as a means of raising emotional interest were contradictory to the task of rendering the historical truth. The conflict can first be seen among the Alexander historians. His exploits were the very subject for a romantic and rhetorical narrative; the earliest writer of this school was Aristotle's nephew Callisthenes (d. 328), who wrote a book of fiction and flattery; others took a similar line, the most influential being the third-century Cleitarchus. He, and the popular tradition which followed him, had a far greater influence than the sober and factual works of some men who had served under Alexander, such as Ptolemy who became king of Egypt, Nearchus the admiral, and Aristobulus. Eventually romantic history turned into the Alexander Romance, a fairy tale of the most fantastic nature, a mixture of Greek and Oriental elements, whose origins belong to the later Hellenistic Age.

There were odd mixtures of factual and fictional history, e.g. in the books of the Babylonian Berossus and the Egyptian Manetho who wrote their native histories for a Greek public. Among Greek historians the contrast between the two types prevailed. The one was again represented by men of sound political or military experience such as Hieronymus of Cardia, Aratus of Sicyon and Polybius. To the other school, called 'tragic history' by Polybius, belonged gossipy writers like Duris and Phylarchus; the latter is expressly criticized by Polybius. He also reproves Timaeus (c. 350–c. 250), the historian of the western Greeks, because of his bookish pedantry; but Timaeus was a serious historian and the type he represents, that of the armchair historian, was to become more and more common. But the real summit of Hellenistic historiography was Polybius. He firmly believed in the usefulness of history for the practical politician. He relied on rational explanations and maintained a markedly ethical attitude; a son of his time, he also paid tribute to the force of Tyche, thus combining two apparently inconsistent elements. But both served his pedagogic aims: one must not only know the facts but also learn from the way men stood up to the blows of fate. Polybius was a fervent admirer of Rome and of his own Achaean league; he can be very unfair to their enemies. He does not reach his own ideal of unbiased truth and falls short of his own standards of accuracy. He is, however, the only extant example after Thucydides of a reliable Greek historian. In describing the Roman constitution (book vi) he puts forward two at first sight incompatible theories, that of the mixed constitution and that of a cycle of constitutions; it is difficult, though not impossible, to unite the two theories as expressions of the permanent ideal and the ever-changing reality. The expansion of the Roman empire is Polybius' general theme; in writing contemporary history, he wrote universal history as well, in a sense in which nobody had done so before. He was not a great writer but a significant figure in historiography. The same Rome he admired, however, was to crush the very spirit he represented.

Polybius' method of writing history approached historical scholarship. Even more scholarly were some of the antiquaries such as the Atthidographers (writers of Athenian chronicles) or Craterus, who edited a collection of Athenian public decrees. Literature and scholarship were closely connected, and the fame (or the notoriety) of the Alexandrians is even more securely based on their scholarship than on their literature. It was they who were responsible for the preservation of many classical works and the establishment of correct or at least readable texts. Then and there, Classical scholarship was born. Its primary object was Homer, whose works were edited by Zenodotus and Aristarchus. The Alexandrians also wrote commentaries which provided most of the material preserved in the *scholia* of later times. We owe to the Alexandrians, among other things, the text and the extant selection of Athenian tragedy and comedy, as made by Aristophanes of Byzantium. The scholars of Alexandria and Pergamum also established the study of language and grammar; an Alexandrian of the second century, Dionysius Thrax, created most of our grammatical terminology. Biography too became a branch of scholarship; a papyrus has preserved part of Satyrus' life of Euripides, written as a dialogue. Many biographies included gossip and scandalmongering; faked letters of famous persons became a popular element in semi-fiction, and many of the anecdotes in Plutarch or Diogenes Laertius go back to Hellenistic writers.

The beginnings of the novel as a special form of art belong to the Hellenistic era. There were romantic love stories which remained famous for many centuries, such as those of Hero and Leander, Pyramus and Thisbe, Sappho and Phaon; and there were also travel stories. The two together were the formative elements of the novel, though some Oriental influence in its creation seems certain; Euhemerus' story (see above) probably showed such influence. Other prose books might deal with the lives of *hetaerae* (courtesans) or the art of cooking or the interpretation of dreams. These books were usually not on a high literary level and with their sentimentalism or their special instruction catered for a wider reading public. It was the same with prose as with poetry.

Literature, scholarship and science worked together in various ways. A central position was held by geography. Its progress was based mainly on two facts: the exploration of Eastern countries in the course of and after Alexander's campaigns, and voyages of discovery like those of Pytheas of Massilia and the Carthaginian Hanno in the Atlantic Ocean; and, on the other hand, the specialization in scientific research in the Peripatetic school. Alexander's surveyors (the 'bematists') had measured a great deal of Asia, and Aristotle's pupil Dicaearchus had made a map of the known world. Eratosthenes (second half of the third century) had a great comprehensive mind; he studied at Athens and then worked at Alexandria. He established the foundations of Greek chronology (improved by his pupil Apollodorus) and wrote on various subjects, but his fame is based on his achievements in mathematical geography. He measured the perimeter of the earth and reached a result close to the one now accepted. He found out a great deal about the shape of the continents, and he wrote a textbook of descriptive geography which had many successors. Polybius had the historian's interest for this kind of work. Poseidonius (c. 135–c. 50), among his many activities, made a study of the Atlantic Ocean and took up the idea, first expressed as a possibility by Eratosthenes, that a comparatively short voyage west would lead to India; the idea survived antiquity and still prevailed in the mind of Christopher Columbus. Finally, Strabo (under the emperor Tiberius) compiled the results of research and description in his *Geography*, an invaluable collection of material and at the same time a work of high literary standing.

For his mathematics Eratosthenes used the *Elements* of Euclid. The logic of this comprehensive textbook of plane and solid geometry, divided as it was into definitions, postulates and axioms, made it truly a work of genius, although it was mainly based on the work of the Pythagoreans and other predecessors. Euclid also did important mathematical research, and he was probably the first to state the value of 'pure science'. A greater mathematician, in fact the greatest among the ancients, was Archimedes, whose work in both pure and applied mathematics, and the variety and depth of whose thought were outstanding. Several of his books have survived. He solved some problems of quadrature, using methods closely related to integration, and he put the exact value of π between very narrow limits. No later mathematicians were of major importance, except Apollonius of Perga with his *Conics*, and perhaps Hipparchus, chiefly an astronomer, who first distinguished trigonometry from geometry. In applying his theories to mechanics, Archimedes became the inventor of various clever devices; e.g. the water screw ('screw of Archimedes'). On the whole the technical, compared with the theoretical, achievements of the age were limited, though less so than is usually assumed. One of the reasons for the lack of technical achievement may have been that cheap labour was ample and there was therefore little need for labour-saving machines; the megalomania of Ptolemy IV and Hieron, on the other hand, could lead to great technical achievements in the building of giant ships. Hero of Alexandria constructed and wrote comprehensively on mechanical devices; he probably belongs to the first century A.D. but he described Hellenistic mechanics. A complicated gearbox, a surprising example of advanced Hellenistic technology, has been recovered from a ship wrecked early in the first century B.C.

In astronomy the Babylonians had prepared the way, and their own astronomy, which had declined into astrology, was revived under Greek influence. There was mutual give and take as in hardly any other matter. Astronomical thought and observation centred on the planetary system. The traditional view had been geocentric; i.e. that sun, moon and planets circled round a stationary earth. Then it emerged that the earth turned on its own axis and also that Venus and Mercury revolved round the sun. Hence Aristarchus of Samos claimed that the sun was larger than the earth and the centre of the whole system. This heliocentric theory, hampered by the assumption that the planets revolved in circles, was almost universally rejected and had to wait until in the sixteenth century Copernicus renewed it. Hipparchus restored the geocentric view, basing it on a complicated system of epicycles (smaller circles within a circular movement round the earth). But he was a great astronomer and was able to measure almost accurately the lunar and solar years. That, however, had no more effect than the theory of Seleucus, a hellenized Babylonian (c. 150 B.C.), who realized that a relation between earth and moon caused the variations of tides. Several astronomers (among them Poseidonius) tried to estimate the sun's diameter and its distance from the earth; they all widely underestimated the true figures. The work achieved in astronomy was summarized – with many errors avoided by earlier men – in the standard book of Ptolemy (c. A.D. 140), who for centuries remained the only authority.

In biology Aristotle's works on zoology and Theophrastus' on botany found few followers even in their own school. This is surprising in view of the rich material provided by Alexander and the hunting expeditions of some of the later kings. Ptolemy II founded a zoo, attached to the Museum. Medicine, on the other hand, made great progress, especially in anatomy and physiology. Dissection of dead bodies became fairly common and surgery was practised with some success. It is doubtful whether experiments on live animals took place. The functions of brain and nerves, of the arteries and their connection with the heart, were traced. By the second century, physicians became more interested in the study of drugs and poisons. Moreover, temple cures and the magic miracles of quacks gained ground over and against scientific medicine.

The Hellenistic Age knew nothing of chemistry and very little of physics or geology. Experiments were rare, except in mechanics, and these were rarely concerned with instruments for practical use, never for scientific research. This fact and the later intellectual development explain the limits of Hellenistic science. Nevertheless, there has been no period before the modern age with such a wide interest in science and scientists as the first two centuries after Alexander the Great. Observation and reasoning combined and achieved remarkable results. Afterward, partly through the lack of instruments and partly because of the retreat of rational methods, a deterioration set in, which eventually brought to a halt all scientific progress.

Hellenistic art, on the other hand, was on the whole a continuation of Classical Greek art, despite the changed conditions and the new tasks for artists and patrons alike. Elegant craftsmanship and emotional strength were generally just as intensely expressed as in literature; architecture shared in the advances of mathematics and engineering. Town planning entered a new phase. The old fifth-century scheme of Hippodamus with its rectangular pattern suited the prevailing rational mind; it was improved and altered according to localities. Water supply and drainage were problems now seriously tackled. Public buildings, usually endowed by a rich citizen or one of the kings, were erected on a large scale; there were fewer temples, but theatres, gymnasia, porticos and colonnades were erected in cities old and new. Of the royal palaces practically nothing is known. Hellenistic towns, though closely built up, showed perhaps more splendour than those of Classical times. Private houses followed previous types, but with more space and adornments. Real innovations in building were rare; the arch, long known in the East, occurred sometimes, but it was the Romans who really used it and revolutionized architecture. Outstanding in Hellenistic times was the building of city walls and fortifications. On the whole, Hellenistic architecture, with its occasional tendency to build on a colossal scale, was impressive and, for example, the acropolis of Pergamum and the colonnaded market places of some cities must have been striking sights.

No branch of art reveals more clearly the spirit of the age than sculpture, if only because so much of it has survived. Many sculptors followed in the paths of the great masters of the fourth century, but to a growing extent new styles developed which, not without good reason, have been called the baroque and rococo of Greek sculpture. Repose became movement, serenity emotion, idealism turned into realism, loveliness into sensuality, tradition into a search for originality. Complicated groups were quite common in the later phases. The demand for sculpture had much increased, and high prices were paid. Portrait statues abounded, and indeed portraiture was one of the great achievements of the time; starting from Lysippus' 'Alexander', statues of kings and statesmen were set up, and also of poets and writers. Fine portraits are also found on gems and coins. Many works showed little more than high craftsmanship; but there were masterpieces such as the 'Victory' of Samothrace, the 'Dying Gaul' or the 'Tyche' of Antioch (Fortune as the city goddess). They belong to the third century, originating from different schools at Rhodes or Pergamum. Later great works were the 'Aphrodite' of Melos (the 'Venus de Milo', now in the Louvre), the 'Aphrodite' of Cyrene in the Terme Museum, Rome, and the heroic so-called 'Hellenistic Ruler', also in Rome. The two latter examples show an overemphasis of feminine sensuality or muscular manliness; while the 'Laocoon' in the Vatican expresses violence of a rather histrionic kind. A work unique in its colossal size and the exuberance of its style is the frieze of the great altar at Pergamum (in the Pergamum Museum, Berlin); the old theme of the battle between gods and giants was probably intended to symbolize the victory of Greek civilization over the barbarians, but with its overcrowding and the turmoil of strange bodies it is almost an example of barbarization itself. The trend towards exaggeration is shown in different ways, for instance in the sweetness of children (Eros is represented as a baby for the first time) or the ugliness of drunken woman.

Reliefs too grew more naturalistic, partly by the use of perspective to distinguish different levels in depth, partly by the combination of sculpture and painting. Of painting practically nothing purely Hellenistic survives. A copy of an early painting is the wonderful Alexander mosaic found at Pompeii which shows great dramatic power and command of composition. Otherwise there are Pompeian wall decorations and frescoes which derive from Hellenistic models but do not simply copy them. Perspective as well as light and shade were used in Hellenistic times, but what the colour schemes were like is not known. Later Hellenistic painters probably used landscape in the manner of some of the Pompeian works. Portrait painting also has left its mark. Vase painting was of little significance, except for new provincial styles and techniques, especially in Italy, which practically ended in the second century B.C. The terracotta statuettes from Tanagra and other places show charmingly realistic scenes of the life of women and children.

So far all Hellenistic art was in the Greek tradition. There is hardly any evidence of Eastern influence, apart from the official continuation of the native tradition in Egypt. Works of a much later date, such as the frescoes from Doura, actually display Eastern influence, but it is not known to what extent they go back to Hellenistic times. The reverse is true where Eastern art is concerned. Many examples show Greek influence on Eastern art. Most remarkable are the 'Greco-Indian' sculptures, chiefly found in Gandhara, among them a type of Buddha which clearly shows its Greek ancestry. The date of these is disputed; they may well begin in the first century A.D. and derive through Parthia from Roman models. From India this mixed art slowly travelled eastward through Turkestan to China. In the West, Carthaginian architects and sculptors copied Hellenistic models. The story of the impact of Greek art on Rome is well known.

Turning now to philosophy, the mental outlook of the third century was optimistic and restless. Men needed guidance in the face of changing conditions. To be no longer the citizen of an independent city-state implied the loss of the traditional bonds of Greek ethics. The aristocratic philosophies of Plato or Aristotle meant very little to the average Greek, and though he still worshipped his old gods they were unable to help him in his daily encounters with the vicissitudes of life. He might believe in fate and be satisfied with a resignation that left his life in the hands of a capricious and inscrutable power. But the demand for new standards of life grew and was met by various kinds of philosophers, all primarily moralists, preaching to the ordianry citizen how to avoid unhappiness and pain. Most spectacular were the Cynics, a sect rather than a school, founded by Diogenes 'the dog'. He lived and preached a life of primitive self-sufficiency. He wrote nothing, but his followers, many of them itinerant preachers like Crates of Thebes, did write both prose and poetry. They developed new literary forms, especially the *diatribe*, a popular sermon, and the satire, usually in verse and often in the form of a parody. Bion of Borysthenes was famous for the former, Menippus of Gadara for the latter; both had started life as slaves. There was a clear anti-bourgeois tendency in the Cynics' writings, but their teaching left the individual in a social vacuum. They also indulged in polemics with other philosophers. One school that drew the most radical conclusions was that of the Sceptics, founded by Pyrrho of Elis. They doubted everything and ended in complete nihilism. Plato's Academy took up a similar attitude later and failed to provide any guidance, while the Peripatetics, the pupils of Aristotle, wavering between isolated scientific disciplines and popular ethics, lost all philosophical originality and influence. Two new schools, however, emerged at Athens, the Epicuraeans and the Stoics, neither any longer concerned with the discovery of truth but with the conduct of the individual in order to reach personal happiness. Their ethics went far beyond the ethics of polis society.

Epicurus, in his teaching and writing, covered the whole field of philosophy, but his real aim was the undisturbed peace of man's soul (*ataraxia*). Freedom from fear, from pain and from emotions was essential. The enjoyment of pleasures was part of human happiness, but only if under such restraint that they did not interfere with man's peace of mind. That equivocal rule could easily be misunderstood and misused; it could lead to outright hedonism, but, on the other hand, enjoyment might just as easily turn into asceticism. Basing his philosophy on Democritus' mechanical atomic doctrine, Epicurus had no interest in its scientific side but used it for a materialistic explanation of emotional life and as the foundation for a remarkable insight into psychosomatic facts. He also used it, as it were, to put religion in cold storage. He did not deny the existence of gods; they were to be honoured by the traditional rites, but only as a group of super-Epicuraeans who lived somewhere outside the world and did not interfere in human life. Epicurus believed in free will as the foundation of morality. The community of 'the garden' was based on mutual friendship and the reverence felt for its founder. His doctrines were never substantially altered, and much of it has come down through enthusiastic followers like Philodemus and the Roman poet Lucretius. Though there were a good many Epicuraeans during the following centuries, not least in Rome, their aversion to active life and lack of interesting politics and rhetoric prevented them from exercising a wide influence. There was, however, a growing desire for retreat from the world and into oneself; Epicurus' teaching, which was really spiritual escapism, made some people very happy.

Of Stoicism, on the other hand, it has been said that it was *the* philosophy of the Hellenistic Age. Founded by a hellenized Phoenician, Zeno, and called after the *stoa* (portico) at Athens where he lectured, Stoicism was to become a truly universal philosophy, though essentially Greek and deeply influenced by Cynic teaching. Subsequent heads of the Stoa were first Cleanthes and later Chrysippus, another Oriental, who gave more logical coherence to the existing body of doctrines. Its earliest ancestor was Heraclitus, whose *logos* was re-established as Providence or Nature, ruling the universe according to eternal laws. The *logos* was claimed to be a material all-pervading spirit (*pneuma*), a dynamic force which provided an ultimate explanation of physical phenomena. It was also the basis of the rational psychology and ethics of Stoicism. They were both individualistic and cosmopolitan. There were no differences between Greek and non-Greek, man and woman, free and slave. The great idea of the brotherhood of men originated from the Stoics; a modern view that it started with Alexander the Great cannot be accepted. It was in every human being's power to gain complete virtue. This ideal of an entirely self-sufficient man (the 'sage') seems almost inhuman; like the Epicuraean ideal, it aimed at an undisturbed peace of mind, but without leaving worldly affairs alone. That ideal was to some extent realized when some Romans accepted Stoic teaching.

In any philosophical religion the gods were little more than accessories. Thus in Stoicism myth was incorporated by allegorical interpretation. Moreover, the rational power or *logos* was divine, a non-anthropomorphic deity, addressed as Zeus in a beautiful hymn by Cleanthes. Whatever its name, whether Zeus or Heimarmene ('Destiny') or Nature, it was all-wise and all-embracing; thus the common belief in Tyche was raised to a higher level. There were inconsistencies in Stoic philosophy, and it is sometimes doubtful to what period of Stoic philosophy certain doctrines belong, for instance whether the idea of a world state (*cosmopolis*) was proclaimed as early as Zeno. In contrast to the Epicuraeans, Stoic philosophy played an important part in public life; some Stoics advised kings and statesmen; one king, Antigonus Gonatas, was a Stoic, and much social reform was due to Stoic initiative. As the embodiment of the highest human potentialities, the Stoics took Heracles who cleansed the world of evil. There was a conflict, never solved in principle, between wisdom and determinism, which only confirms that Stoicism came near to being a religion. With its strict moralism, it offered mankind a guidance which was widely accepted. Rome received it in a watered-down form through Panaetius and Poseidonius (the so-called 'Middle Stoa' school). The latter, a forceful and versatile thinker, combined the most various branches of science and scholarship with Stoic doctrine. His books are lost and to what extent they were used by Cicero and others is much disputed. It seems certain that he differed from the school tradition by introducing mystical and eschatological elements. The later Stoics – represented under the empire by Seneca, Epictetus and the emperor Marcus Aurelius – returned to what has been called 'a religion of the educated' but was essentially a rather trivial refuge in a disturbed world.

In this context, on the borderline of philosophy and religion, it seems appropriate to deal with the relations between Greeks and Jews. These relations, though only part of the larger relations between East and West, are of particular importance, first because the Jews were the only people who opposed Greek civilization on principle, and second because their mutual influence was all-important for the origin of Christianity. During the third century the tiny community of Judaea, ruled by a high priest, was under Ptolemaic sovereignty but hardly figured in history. For a long time the Greeks knew very little about the Jews, although the number of Jews living in communities outside Judaea (the Jews of the Dispersion) gradually increased and some Greek writers had a vague concept of Jewish monotheism. A section of the Judaean Jews, however, had begun to adopt Greek ways of life, and it was this upper class that turned to the Seleucids when they became masters of Palestine c. 200. The Hellenizers were strongly opposed by the mass of the people. The climax came under Antiochus IV Epiphanes. It is disputed whether he was moved to his interference by a previous revolt and simply acted to recreate a strong Seleucid government, or whether his aim was to spread hellenization. The cult of Olympian Zeus introduced by Antiochus into the Temple was in fact that of a Syrian Baal in Greek disguise. Antiochus certainly sided with the hellenized upper class against the people who were perhaps first led by the *Hasidim* ('pious'), finally by the Hasmonaean family, also known as the Maccabees. The war of the Maccabees eventually saved Judaism, but the independent state which emerged showed increasingly Hellenistic features and underwent a process of secularization culminating in the rule of the Idumaean Herod the Great.

Jewish literature flourished during the second and first centuries, showing Greek influence in varying degrees. There are for example the two historical books of *Maccabees*, witnesses of extreme nationalism, of which the second was originally written in Greek. Others were added either to the canonical or the apocryphal books of the Old Testament. The author of the *Book of Wisdom* knew Greek logical terms and may have read Plato; the skepticism and pessimism of *Ecclesiastes* was hardly possible without Hellenistic philosophy, nor the *Song of Solomon* without Hellenistic love poetry. Yet direct borrowing is doubtful. The decisive factor was that Jews and Greeks were contemporaries in the same world. Much of this Jewish literature was written outside Judaea, and naturally Greek influence was strongest in the Dispersion. Jewish communities with their synagogues could be found all over the Hellenistic world, and in some cities they were acknowledged as a separate *politeuma*. Many Jews took Greek names and imitated Greek ways; some even seem to have worshipped the 'Highest God' or Zeus Sabazius, who was identified with the Lord Sabaoth. Many no longer knew Hebrew or Aramaic but only Greek, and it was for their sake (though with much more far-reaching effects) that in Egypt the Greek translation of the Old Testament known as the Septuagint was made. Most Jewish books of the time had little influence on the further development of Judaism; they were remembered mainly by the Christian church. The prevailing traditionalism of the Jews in Judaea and the religious customs of Jewish life everywhere excluded close intercourse with the Greeks. No Jew could really worship the city gods. Anti-Semitism began to develop, partly because of economic rivalry but mainly through mutual religious propaganda and because the Jews, though active in all sorts of professions, were different from other people and kept apart. The important Jewish community at Alexandria never gained citizenship as such; only individuals, who more or less gave up their religion, were truly hellenized.

The influence was by no means only in one direction. The Jews of the Dispersion began to win proselytes (as can be seen in the book of *Jonah*, though that may belong to an earlier period), and even without that some Greeks were prepared to learn from Jewish tradition. In the attempts to make philosophy the handmaid of religion, the revelations of Eastern religions, and in particular of Jewish monotheism, were regarded as means of gaining the knowledge (*gnosis*) which would lead man to immortality. Influence of the Old Testament and later Jewish writings can be traced, for instance, in the *Hermetica* (occult writings supposed to derive from Hermes Trismegistos), especially the *Poimandres*. Quite a different example of a union between Jewish religion and Greek philosophy is provided by Philo of Alexandria, who lived under the early empire but whose books are truly Hellenistic. He tried to explain the Old Testament by allegorical interpretation, a method well known in Hellenistic thought. His speculations did not markedly affect the development of Palestinian Judaism but were contributions of primary importance to Christian theology. Other significant developments among the Jews were the teaching of the Essenes, a monastic brotherhood, and the hope of the coming of the Messiah.

All this is part of a more general story. Jewish beliefs in the Hellenistic era had much in common with other forms of worship. In a sense the Hellenistic development culminated in the victory of religion. In the term 'religion' all sorts of irrational beliefs and superstitions, often hidden in pseudo-scientific disguise, are included. The ancient Greek religion was by no means dead, but it was not able to serve the needs of people who longed for personal help and happiness and for the security of an afterlife. Fear of death had an integral part in many of the people's beliefs. What a minority found in the teaching of philosophers was looked for by most people in various forms of worship, in astrology or in magic and occult practices. This was not only a spiritual but also a social movement; in the end the uneducated masses, but not they alone, got what they wanted and needed.

Certain forms of religion had always been strong in the East and continued to be so in the Hellenistic Age. The Hellenistic rulers with very few exceptions exercised religious tolerance, though they fought the power of the priests. As to Greek religion, there is evidence not only of constant and even intensified public worship, but also of a new importance of some members of the traditional Pantheon. Among these were Asclepius, the healing god, for example, with his cures effected by sleeping in his temple at Epidaurus, and, above all, Dionysus as the god of mystic and ecstatic worship. The door was open for more personal forms of religion, which at the same time were universal. The differences between the gods gradually disappeared and additional names like *Soter* ('saviour') could be more important than their real names. Polytheism was on its way towards monotheism. Moreover, the Greeks had always assimilated foreign deities to their own and in this process they frequently changed their nature. During the Hellenistic Age, Greek and Eastern forms of worship were united in widespread fusion which is called syncretism. It played its part in the ruler cult and in the belief in Tyche as mere Chance, who was assimilated to Cybele and Isis; it served to reshape Oriental cults in order to satisfy Greek believers; it was active in the artificial creation of Sarapis (Serapis) by Ptolemy I and in the growing diffusion of the cults of the Syrian and Egyptian gods, none more spectacular than that of Isis who, together with Sarapis, became the centre of an organized and truly universal religion.

The deeper reason for this success is probably that the cult of Isis – as of several other deities – included mysteries which would bring some certainty of salvation to the initiate. The Greeks had their own mysteries, like those of Eleusis and Orphism, both still going strong. Mysteries of Dionysus flourished. The Eastern cults, however, more drastic, more savage, gained ground, though the full impact did not reach Greeks and Romans before the first century A.D. The story enacted in the mystery might deal with the death and resurrection of a god, or with a divine marriage, but the real theme was death and afterlife – that is to say, the victory of life over death. By the process of initiation, which might take a long time and could include ascetic life, confession, baptism and sacraments, the individual was gradually raised to higher levels of purity and perfection, and finally reached redemption and immortality; sometimes this meant a kind of rebirth. In the Great Mother of the Gods and in Isis the ancient mother goddess of pre-Greek times had a triumphant revival. It can hardly be denied that she lives on in the concept of the Christian Virgin and Child.

Mystery religions were bound to restrict the number of their adherents; besides, the demands made on the individual were not for everybody. There were easier ways to approach the supernatural and to overcome the fear of unguided freedom. One was astrology, invented centuries earlier in Babylon. It was based on the concept of star worship, and it meant belief in the connection between human life and the laws of the sky. Either the seven planets or the twelve signs of the zodiac governed the lives of men and states alike, and the casting of horoscopes became a means of foretelling the future; but astrologists were not interested in eschatological ideas. Astrology could lead to a disastrous fatalism, and people tried various ways of escape. One of these was magic, which came from the East and in Hellenistic times had its centre in Egypt. All sorts of magic beliefs and practices spread, together with the belief in beings between man and god, who, good or more likely evil, might be induced to serve man. These *daemones* were approached by magic methods as various and plentiful as there were wandering magicians and trusting believers.

Hellenistic civilization, as every great civilization, had very varied aspects. While preserving the Greek heritage, and at the same time spreading it wide and far, Hellenistic man discovered new ways of thought, of belief and of life. State and society, literature, art and science, philosophy and religion, all bear witness to an atmosphere that was different from earlier and later times. At the end of the era, there are two gigantic phenomena, the creation of the Roman empire and the advent of Christianity. Although both drew their main strength from other sources, in many of their features they can be seen as having evolved from the Hellenistic Age.

7

Some Roman concepts of state and empire[1]

The title of this paper sounds vague. It really can't be otherwise. If I am trying to speak of political concepts of the Romans I have to select a few out of an almost numberless crowd. I trust it is clear that I am not going to speak of institutions. I have indicated my main principle of selection by confining my subject to *concepts* of state and empire. That is to say that I shall say very little, if anything, about the well-known slogans of Roman political and social life, such as *amicitia*, *clientela*, *factio*, or even *fides*, *dignitas*, *auctoritas*, *clementia* or *libertas*, though I shall have to mention them. All have been frequently treated, and, of course, they are all most important if one wishes to study the political mind of the Romans. In confining myself, as far as possible, to a much more limited theme, I hope at least to avoid being too lengthy and superficial.

The two words state and empire derive from Latin; but *status* is hardly ever used independently in a political sense; it means something like condition or state of affairs or constitutional structure when Cicero and others frequently mention the *status rei publicae* or the *status civitatis*; as we speak of the 'state of the Union', later authors could speak of the *status Romanus*, and thus bridge the gulf to our word 'state' in its specific meaning. Empire, i.e. *imperium*,

[1] Unpublished lecture delivered as the Lily Ross Taylor lecture at Bryn Mawr College in 1962.

is of a different kind. We shall have to deal with it in more detail; it is well known that the word underwent a long process of development before it acquired the meaning of empire. In a way, the Romans had no words which exactly correspond to the English expression. British people should well understand that. French *état* and German *Staat* have an emotional force which English 'state' has not. There is (or rather was) a strong feeling about the word and concept of empire and then of Commonwealth; but at home the British speak of England, Wales or Scotland, possibly of the United Kingdom, and never of the British state. In the United States the word state has become the technical term for the members of the Union; for the whole federation as far as I know, neither state nor – still less – empire are possible expressions.

However, we shall not be able to speak of our subject without using the concept of state. Thus, we first concentrate on *res publica* which beyond doubt is the nearest in Latin to it. Hence our word Republic, which would imply that *res publica* is only the free, the unmonarchical state. It is a common habit to refer to the centuries before Augustus as the period of the *res publica*, and to the succeeding centuries as that of the empire. But there was an empire before Augustus, and as late as the sixth century A.D. people would still call the Roman state a *res publica*, even in the determined meaning of *civitas libera*. A gold medal of Maxentius, an opponent of Constantine, has the legend: *Liberator rei publicae*. There was no clear demarcation line in Rome between the eras of the Republic and of monarchy. The day when Octavian proclaimed the *r. p. restituta*, the Ides of January 27 B.C., is commonly and, I think, rightly regarded as the birthday of the Principate, and the Principate started, to put it as simply as possible, as a monarchy in republican forms, rather than a conventional monarchy. On the other hand, the distinction between a republican and an imperial period is not really mistaken, and Tacitus was the first to make the distinction. He was no republican; yet he felt the essential change which took place when Augustus became princeps. Sir Ronald Syme has reminded us that the principal contestants on both sides belonged to the same class, but he also claims that the Republic died hard, that is to say, it did die. The turn from republican *libertas* to *obsequium* (*ruere in servitium consules patres eques*)[2] meant less a constitutional matter than one of social change and of personal attitude in the face of despotism. It is remarkable that Tacitus as well as Pliny found *libertas* restored under Trajan's benevolent absolutism.

You see there is still a good deal to be done, if it can be done at all, to discover what really was in the mind of the Romans, and my remarks today should be understood as a small contribution to that end. I shall quote some of our sources, but I shall not discuss modern literature, though I wish to express my thanks to many scholars to whose writings I am indebted. I shall discuss a few Latin words and ideas the meaning of which is not so obvious that it would be sufficient to look them up in Lewis and Short, or in the Thesaurus. At the same time, I wish to emphasize once and for all that all these concepts are neither rigidly fixed in themselves nor rigidly separated from one another.

We naturally begin with the word already mentioned, with *res publica*. It is composed of a noun and an adjective: *res*, usually in the singular, is a collective, indicating any general matter which is frequently explained by an adjective – *res militaris, res rustica, res privata, res familiaris, res divina*. Instead of the collective singular the same expression can also appear in plural, but it is the collective meaning that counts. In contrast to the Greek polis, *res* could not act; all political business was done by S.P.Q.R. and more directly by the magistrates. *Senatus magistratus leges* is the formula. The meaning of *res* comprehends all sorts of things, from the most concrete matter like property (*rem facere* – to make money) to more abstract concepts such as 'interest' (Plaut. *Amphitryo* 9: *ea uti nuntiem quae maxume in rem vestram communem sient* – announcing what may most contribute to your common good). Or Cicero (*rep.* 1, 60) speaks of *res* transferred to many within the *res publica*; that is to say, *res* can be something like the power in the state (think of *rerum potiri*!). We also have: *rem gerere* or *rem bene gerere*, which was used for public, especially military action. The office of dictatorship, when no special duty was involved, was legally described as *dictatura rei gerendae*. The plural could, of course, refer to a number of events. The *res bene gestae* were quoted for giving reasons for a

[2] 'Consuls, senators, knights, all rushed into servitude' (Tac. *ann.* 1, 7).

triumph (cf. Mummius *ILS* 20, 146 B.C.). The *res gestae* as Rome's past history meant something as close to the heart of the people as the deeds of their ancestors to that of every noble family.

Whatever else *res* can mean, as *res publica* it is concerned with public affairs, whether it refers to general conditions or possessions (as for example in *rem publicam augere*), or the more or less abstract concept of the political community. What that implies Cicero tells us in *de leg.* (5, 41): a senator must know the *res publica*, and that includes strength of the army, value of treasury, allies, friends, tributaries, laws, stipulations, treaties. This is a dry enumeration, and few senators would have been up to it. But in including and even stressing the part played by dependent and foreign countries, and this involving what we would call the empire, there is a clear feeling of the greatness of the *res publica*. This emotional element comes fully into the open when Cicero at several occasions (e.g. at the beginning of the third and at the end of the fourth Catilinarian) makes *res publica* the highest scale of values which, in slightly varied order but with equal emphasis, starts from the life and family of each citizen and progresses to the temples and altars, to *urbs* and *civitas* and finally *res publica*. It is *sanctissimum nomen*, and it is the ultimate proof of good citizenship to die *pro re publica*, a sentence on the same emotional level as Horace's *dulce et decorum est pro patria mori*.

Cicero (in *de rep.*) several times defines *res publica* as *res populi*. This looks as if it might be influenced by Greek philosophy. In fact, however, we find it was an old and current Roman notion: *publicus* (earlier: *poplicus*) is simply the adjective belonging to *populus* (e.g. in Plaut. *Truc.* 56: in *re populi placida et otiosa*, 'when public life is quiet and lazy'). The *res populi* was the *res publica*, largely its social as contrasted with the political aspect, with all its different meanings, and it confirms the personal implications of the whole expression. We turn to *populus*. Its etymology is unknown. It was any group of people living together as a community. It can be the same as village or town. The *triginta populi* were the communities of Latium, the earliest Latin confederation with which Rome had to deal. Rome herself grew together from several such villages when she was under the rule of the Etruscan kings, probably in the late seventh century. That was the true foundation of Rome. At the same time, we must not forget that a *populus* is primarily a social or even a military, not a political body, and that meant in Rome a number of noble families, organized in *curiae*. After they were replaced by the *centuriae* and the aristocratic by the military division, the *populus Romanus* included all those who as citizens would fight for the *res publica*. In that sense, *populus Romanus* was an equivalent of the Roman state. What was the difference between *res publica* and *populus Romanus*? To Cicero, they were the same. It meant no rule by a section, whether a tyrant, an oligarchy, or the masses. We realize the theoretical character of Cicero's definition. The *res publica* was more than a body of men, however organized, though it existed by and for the *p. R.* The *res publica* was the roof over the total of *cives Romani*, whether these were few or many. The empire could develop under this roof. It was not, as we have seen, a mere abstract; it could even be thought of as a living body itself; Cicero speaks of *rei publicae sanguis* or *corpus*. Still, that was metaphorical use. The *res publica* was never regarded as an acting person and was never deified.

No definition, however, seems quite satisfactory, and neither *res publica* nor *populus Romanus* fully covered the concept of state. That is the reason why often accumulation occurred, as in the censors' call to the citizens, almost a prayer, to assemble on the Campus Martius (Varro, *de ling. lat.* (6, 86): *quod bonum fortunatum felix salutareque siet populo Rom. Quiritium reique publicae populi Romani Quiritium mihique collegaeque meo, fidei magistratuique nostro*. However, as a fixed and separate expression, *res publica* was something more than the *populus Romanus*. It was more than a community, because it was every matter and the whole matter that concerned the community. Even so, it was at first simply the opposite to *res privata*. We read, for example in Plautus (*Pers. 65*), that a man was praised because he had in his mind the public interest rather than his own (*publicae rei causa id facit magis quam sui quaesti*). Or in another passage somebody says: 'Am I not a fool *qui rem curo publicam ubi sint magistratus quos curare oporteat?*' The man in the street does not think that the *res publica* is really his business. It is something similar when we find *res publica* connected with *epitheta*

ornantia, as for example *magna res publica*, which means important
public affairs. Or Plautus again: 'Never mind the young men, but
when old men associate with harlots, where then is room for *res
summa nostra publica*?' The expression *summa res publica* is only a
variation of that frequent and more general phrase *summa rerum*
(also *res* or *rei*), but *summa res publica* is used in a most important
official formula, as in Cicero, *Cat.* 3, 13: *iudiciis expositis atque
editis, Quirites, senatum consului de summa re publica quid fieri placeret.*
Here, *res publica* is truly one concept, is fact: *res populi Romani*, and
we may call it 'state'.

We are back at *populus*. You know the earlier title of the dictator:
magister populi. Magister is the superior, the bearer of public power –
magistratus; minister is the inferior, the attendants (nowadays things
are rather the other way round). *Magister populi* is the leader of the
people in arms, the only magistrate with unlimited power, a temporary successor to the kings. His appointment was a constitutional
means of dealing with an emergency. In early Rome, after the
kings, the magistrates were the executives of the people. But who
was this *populus Romanus*? Cicero's matter-of-fact and yet theoretical definition is (*rep.* 1, 39): *coetus multitudinis iuris consensu et
utilitatis communione sociatus* – a union based on the common
acknowledgement of law and the common pursuit of interest. I
fear this definition, which in English almost sounds as if it were part
of the American Declaration of Independence, cannot help us much.
The *populus* was originally the sum total of the *gentes*, the clans, of
Rome, including patrician and plebeian families. With the end of
the Struggle of the Orders (367) the unity of the *populus* and the *res
publica* was constitutionally established; the *populus Romanus* was
the community of patricians and plebeians, the theoretical sovereign
who elected the magistrates, and who was advised and directed by
the senate and the higher magistrates. Then the *res publica* seemed
really *res populi* though it never was a democracy, never the rule
by the people, but in principle always the rule *for* the people, a state
that by its very nature was aristocratic, but in that respect – like
Greek *politeia* – not bound to a definite form of constitution.
Polybius saw in his idealized Rome, in the combination of S.P.Q.R.
and the power of the magistrates, the ideal mixture of the three

fundamental constitutional forms. For the Romans themselves the *res publica* was the *res publica maiorum*. Even so, reality was different. For several centuries, the government was in the hands of a few families with very few *homines novi* thrown in. It is possible to disagree on the nature of the factors which divided the aristocracy, but both the parts and the total were facts, whatever the effects on the voting of their supporters may have been. The rule of an aristocracy made the *res publica* a state in which elected magistrates, though combining civil and military competences, were restricted in power by various factors such as collegiality, *intercessio* by a colleague or a tribune, time limit, the traditions of the *mos maiorum* (Rome's unwritten laws), and above all the *ius provocationis*, the right of every citizen to appeal to the people against any decision of a magistrate. This was the state in which, in the words of F. E. Adcock, 'the *dignitas* of the great man did not, or should not, deny the *libertas* of the small man'; the state of *auctoritas principum*, *consensus omnium*, or whatever beautiful words were found; the state whose policy was made by the senate, though carried out by the magistrates; the state which according to Cicero existed in the second century, but was lost in the age of Pompey and Caesar. Cicero (*rep.* 5, 2) says: '*rem publicam verbo retinemus, re ipsa vere iam pridem amisimus*' (we shall retain the *res publica* as a word, but have lost the thing itself long ago). The emotional tone of this statement is obvious. Augustus could put forward the counter-claim of the *res publica restituta*; even Cicero himself had spoken (*rep.* 3, 47) of *popularis*, or *regalis*, *res publica*, and the aristocrat Tiberius could still say: '*principes mortales, rem p. aeternam esse*' (Tac. *ann.* 3, 6, 3). Instead of *res publica* one could also speak of *res Romana*. It is especially frequent in Livy, but much earlier Ennius distinguished between *res Romana* as the Roman state and Latium as the Latin confederacy. It was he who wrote the famous line: *moribus antiquis res stat Romana virisque*. The phrase *res Romana*, expressing Roman pride, stressed the Roman character of the state over and against other states; that is probably the reason why it was still frequently used by Ammianus Marcellinus in the fourth century A.D. Normally we should translate it simply by 'Rome'.

But Rome was above all a city: *urbs Roma*. Originally, Rome

Man, State and Deity

was not even a city-state, but just a city. Whether that was *Roma quadrata*, or the town of the seven hills, or the community of the four regions, does not concern us now. The decisive point is that the city, an agrarian community without hinterland, was the place of *all* public business. Its boundaries were fixed at an early time by the sacred furrow of the *pomerium* which originally, it seems, did not even include the *arx*, the hill of the Capitol. The *pomerium*, for all times to come, divided Roman public affairs into the two fundamental areas *domi* and *militiae*. When Rome first expanded, it included the *ager Romanus*, Roman territory of very small size (part of the Campagna). It was not really part of the *res publica* which remained based exclusively on the city; though domestic public affairs were often called *res urbanae*. When the territory grew further, there was no name for it, and that is significant. The only way of describing it was to speak of its *fines*, its boundaries. When new territory in Italy was conquered, it became, as far as it was incorporated, *ager publicus*, land of the *populus Romanus*. There were now *cives* living outside the city, the *urbs*. They had to be roped in into the state organization, and that was done by adding rural *tribus* (eventually thirty-one) to the four urban *tribus*. That was a fairly long process by which Rome, after all, became a city-state, and looked almost, though never quite, like a Greek polis.

I need not remind you of the part the *ager publicus* played in the agrarian laws of the Gracchan revolution. I only quote the famous inscription usually ascribed to Popilius Laenas, enumerating his achievements (*ILS* 23): *Primus fecei ut de agro poplico aratoribus cederent pastores*. One of the chief opponents of the Gracchi, he continued their work although not a member of the commission of the *IIIviri agris distribuendis adsignandis*; thus he could claim that he changed the *ager publicus* from pasture to ploughed land. The urgency of land reform was beyond personal or party strife, because on it depended Roman military power as well as the loyalty of the masses.

The Roman state, for which there was no adequate name, grew beyond its own territory. The story of the conquest of Italy is outside our theme, but in order to understand the development of the state, it is necessary to mention, at least briefly, the forms in which foreign tribes and foreign territories were attached to Rome. It was a process of slow change, and peoples outside Rome could become incorporated or attached in a number of different ways and different degrees of incorporation, from citizenship to *cives sine suffragio*, to *coloniae* and *socii* and *civitates liberae et foederatae*, and provinces. They represent procedures of greater or lesser subtlety, different at different stages and different from each other, though sometimes overlapping. They reached from the 'made Romans' (*facti Romani*) of early times – individual foreigners who were granted citizenship – to the *municipia* and *coloniae* and the various types of *socii*. In such terms, that is to say: in the gradual and graded extension of Roman citizenship, the whole history of the expansion of Rome, of the building-up of her empire, is indicated.

Even after 89 B.C., when the Roman state included the whole peninsula and there was no longer a city-state, the *urbs* remained the centre, even the essence of the state. The *urbs Roma* stands at the core of the writings of the annalists. It was in the centre of Roman political thought no less than action. Our chief witness is, of course, Cicero, and the nature of the man and his writings makes him a reliable witness, if we do not neglect the particular circumstances. I mention a few selected passages. The demand of the *lex Rullia* to colonize the *ager Campanus* was turned by the irate new consul of 63 into an attempt to create in Capua a second Rome.[3] Cicero states that Rome is 'the common fatherland of all of us', and, as he says somewhere else, the only one – and he is, of course, an Italian by birth. The idea that the *res publica* of a city like Capua could become home and heart of the empire (*domicilium imperio*) is one of the ludicrous exaggerations of this speech; but it is obvious: what is ascribed to Capua was true of Rome. We shall return to the concept of *imperium* later on. It is clear from this and other passages that for Cicero Rome represented the state. If he did hardly think of the empire, that is to say, of the provinces as part of the

[3] Cic. *de leg. agr.* 2, 86: *tunc contra hanc Romam, communem patriam omnium nostrum, illa altera quaeretur* – cf. 1. 19: *maiores nostri Capua magistratus, senatum, consilium commune, omnia denique insignia rei publicae sustulerunt, necque aliud quicquam in urbe nisi inane nomen Capuae reliquerunt ... videbant si quod rei publicae vestigium illis moenibus contineretur, urbem ipsam imperio domicilium praebere posse.*

state, others who were, if anything, more rigid in this respect than he, would hold still narrower views.[4] Politics and any man's career were made in Rome and nowhere else. That was the typical way, while the careers of Pompey and Caesar were not. Cicero was horrified when Pompey in 49 evacuated Rome. It was, he writes to Atticus (7, 11, 3), like abandoning the *res publica*, like having Rome destroyed again by the Gauls. Emigration, even with the hope of return, was no solution for him. In exile he was so unhappy that he lost all dignity and constantly implored friends and enemies alike to call him back. It was fundamentally the same later in 51 when he was governor of Cilicia. He was a wise, conscientious, humane governor. But he regarded his task as *labor* and *molestia*, and was afraid his term of office might be extended: *hic ne quid mihi prorogetur . . . horreo (ad. Att. 5, 21, 5)*. More honest than most of his fellow governors, he was still too weak to break with the corrupt system. He gave way to the requests and intrigues of important men in Rome, and provided no protection for the provincials against exploitation, though his famous letter to his brother Quintus shows that he could give sensible advice on how to behave as a provincial governor. It was natural for him to see especially in the Greeks (*ex hominum omni genere humanissimum*) – despite the *Graeculi* of his day – more than mere objects of Roman rule. The same theme occurs again in the younger Pliny's letter of advice (8, 24); the Greeks were referred to by an even more suggestive phrase: *homines maxime homines*. But few Romans felt that way.

There was a fundamental incapacity to rule an empire; that was the other side of the Rome-centredness, of the narrow patriotism, of the Romans. They had to learn to be imperialists. Many never realized that rule over foreign peoples involved duties. If the republican government, the government by a city, did not work even worse than it did, the reason lies largely outside legal institutions. The *res publica* was not only a constitutional framework but from top to bottom (or from the centre to the borders) a complex system of patronage and clientele, *amicitia* and *hospitium*.

---

[4] Cic. *pro Plancio* (54 B.C.), 63: *ita multa Romae geruntur ut vix eaquae fiunt in provinciis audiantur*. 66: . . . *ut etiam summa res publica mihi domi fuerit gerenda et urbs in urbe servanda*.

Some Roman concepts of state and empire

The original *patronus* was the *pater* (just as *matrona* belongs to *mater*), the *pater familias*, and the *familia* included the *clientes*. Hence derive the *patres gentium*, the *patres* as the senate, the patricians as *patris filii* and later the *pater patriae*. In the last phrase, the family concept is doubled; *res publica* could become *patria*, and the bond among the community was *pietas* rather than *amor*. Relationships which originally belonged to families, clans and individuals *within* the state could be extended to people outside and thus become relationships *with* the state. Foreign individuals, communities or states could become clients or *amici populi Romani*; as a relation between a big power and a minor one, *amicitia* was almost identical with *clientela*. As early as the laws of the XII Tablets, the duty of the *patronus* became a matter of law, and sacred law at that: *patronus si clienti fraudem fecerit sacer esto* (if a patron deceives his client he shall be accursed). The quality requested of the *patronus* was *fides* – trust, protection, a guarantee that power was not to be misused, to which the client would react by loyalty and attachment (also *fides*), just as it determined the relations between the Romans and their gods. The concept of *fides* was also the very bond by which a Roman public figure felt compelled to serve the public interest. It was the moderating brake on power and prestige, on *potestas* and *auctoritas*. *Pax* and *fides* belonged together; *fides* was the religious and social basis of Roman rule. Patronage, later extended to the *socii*, was the instrument for the rule of the nobility. It was based on facts of power, wealth, influence, tradition, but also moral obligation with strong religious implications behind it. The system appealed to the very best in Roman conscience; they never thought of a bureaucracy to administer the provinces, and the system survived all constitutional changes. We find that later emperors, members of the imperial family, imperial officials, and individuals of rank and wealth, took over what once had been the privilege of Rome's old aristocratic families.

Let us return once more to Cicero. There is plenty of evidence in his speeches and letters that to him *urbs* was *patria*. Somehow then *tota Italia* belonged to it, as Cato Censorius had seen long before. Cicero's famous formula for his policy was: *tota Italia et concordia ordinum*, the concord of the three classes (senate, equites, plebs) throughout all Italy. Yet the order of 89 remained problematical. Rome was not yet a national state, and no longer a city-state. In practice no way was found to give the Italians an active share in politics. They were citizens, no longer *peregrini*, but it would be a mistake to speak, at that time, of an Italian nation as a political unit. There was the idea of Italy in Roman minds, an unpolitical idea, an emotion rather than a national concept, illustrated by such writers as Varro and Virgil. Cicero's *consensus omnium* was based on that idea, but excluded the Transpadani of North Italy. After Caesar had shown the way, it did include them; but even when they were part of Italy, Cicero (*Phil.* V. 24) could describe them in such equivocal terms as *provincia firmissimorum et fortissimorum civium*, 'the province of the strongest and bravest citizens', but still a province!

The facts of provincial administration under the Republic are, on the whole, well known. Members of the Roman nobility, ex-consuls or ex-praetors, went out in turn for a year, rarely for an extended term, each time with a new staff and with little knowledge of the country concerned and its population. It was a completely inhuman system, an expression of Roman ineptitude in all affairs outside the *res publica*, mitigated only by the possible wisdom and humanity of the governor. The system represents a remarkable paradox: the people, or at least its ruling aristocracy, though more concerned with moral values than possibly any other, abandoned these values when facing the demands of imperial rule.

It needed the complete administrative change under the Principate to make the system really work. The evils of the system under the senate's rule were manifest; but that was not the whole story. The provinces, the *praedia populi Romani*, were also, as I have indicated, the field of *patrocinium*, of patronage. Rome had received the conquered *in fidem populi Romani* and that *fides* was exercised by very many channels of patronage, usually hereditary and competitive among the noble Roman clans. Cicero, ever since the Verrinae of 70 B.C. regarded *patrocinium* as a higher form of government, compared with *imperium*. The praetor C. Claudius Pulcher (*Verr.* 2, 122) decided on a petition by the people of Halaesa in Sicily, not on the strength of his *imperium*, but *de sententia* of all the members of the *gens Metella*, their patrons. The whole *populus Romanus* could be understood as the patron of the provinces, but as the governors held an *imperium populi Romani* a conflict arose between *imperium* and *patrocinium*, between official and unofficial power. Still, a solution, as viewed by Cicero under ideal conditions, was not merely wishful thinking. Roman foreign policy stood under certain religious laws, such as the commandment to wage only a *iustum bellum*. At Cicero's time this practically belonged to a distant past, but we all know how certain political phrases, though emptied of their original force and truth, can still exercise strong power over the minds of the people. Moreover, there was a very real reason for using *patrocinium* rather than *imperium* to rule foreign peoples. Things would usually go much more smoothly, and clientele provided a welcome alternative to annexation. Rome was *lux orbis terrarum et arx omnium gentium*, 'the light of the world and the refuge of all its peoples' (Cic. *Cat.* 4, 6), that is to say, the provinces, and we may add: the *civitates liberae* and the *amici populi Romani* as well being her protectorate.

It is time to ask whether there was a name for it. Neither *res publica* nor *patrocinium* really contained the concept of empire. Both words did survive into imperial times, the one associated with the *libertas senatus* and revered as a relic, or the dishonest fake of the Principate, but virtually meaningless, the other only after changing its nature. The words empire and emperor and some of the passages quoted lead us to the word *imperium*. It had begun sometimes to replace *res publica*; the transition is indicated in the peculiar phrase on the wide rule of Rome (Cic. *rep.* 5, 1): *tanta et tam fuse lateque imperans res publica. Imperium*, the right and power to give orders (military or otherwise) to free citizens, was the *potestas* of the king, the dictator, the praetors, therefore also of the pro-consuls and pro-praetors. It was *imperium populi Romani*, the highest magisterial power held and granted by the people. The pro-magistrates carried it with them to govern their provinces. The word never quite lost its military character, and it grew in strength when the armies and their generals did the same. Thus, under the principate, S.P.Q.R., in Tacitus' significant quip, became: *senatus milesque et populus* (1, 7, 2). *Imperium populi Romani* meant Roman rule, exercised by the magistrates and legions, and soon the geographical extent of that rule. As early as 184 B.C., the elder Africanus, in that famous scene when a tribune accused him of having been bribed by Antiochus, broke up the trial by reminding the people that the day was the anniversary of Zama when he had defeated *Hannibalem imperio vestro inimicissimum*, 'the greatest enemy of your *imperium*' (Gell. 4, 18). Cato (*orig.* 95b), in his speech for the Rhodians, speaks of their fear of servitude under Roman *imperium* (*ne sub solo imperio nostro in servitute nostra essent*). The word is oscillating between the meanings of Roman rule and Roman empire. During the second century B.C. the Romans grew conscious of the fact that they ruled most of the known world, and a phrase of Tiberius Gracchus is preserved, calling the Romans the conqueror of the peoples and the owner of the world (*populus gentium victor orbisque possessor*). The *Rhetorica ad Herennium* speaks of the madness of the Italian *socii* to revolt and to challenge Roman power to which 'all peoples, kings, nations had submitted, either by force or voluntarily'.[5] With increasing clarity there emerged a consciousness of the fact, though not of the obligations, of an empire. Solemnly Cicero, at the end of his first Catilinarian speech, exclaims: *Tu Iuppiter* ... *quem statorem* (the supporter) *huius urbis atque imperii vere nominamus*. In *Somnium Scipionis* (*de rep.* 6, 16) he describes Scipio as looking down from some point in the cosmos, when *imperium nostrum* was little more than a spot (*quasi punctum*) on a very small earth – a remarkable prophecy of space travel! *Urbs et imperium* – it seems as though the *res publica* is beginning to disappear behind these concepts.

It was not a far step from the *imperium populi Romani* to the *Imperium Romanum*, especially after the expression was used for the geographical complex. The frequent phrase *fines imperii propagare* shows the transition from the one to the other. In 49, Caesar wrote a letter to a friend of Pompey (B.C. 3, 57) that he should persuade Pompey to come to terms; then he would earn the credit for provid-

---

[5] *Rhet. ad Herenn.* IV 9, 13: *qui pro nobis pugnare et imperium nobiscum* ... *conservare soliti sunt* ... *nedum illi imperium orbis terrae, cui imperio omnes gentes, reges, nationes partim vi, partim voluntate concesserunt* ... *ad se transferre tantulis viribus conarentur.*

ing *quietem Italiae, pacem provinciarum, salutem imperii.* Salvation of
the empire by peace and unity: the Augustan Age is foreshadowed.
Under Augustus, we have plenty of evidence, also in his *Res Gestae*,
that *imperium* means the empire. Virgil and Horace realized that a
new epoch began with Augustus: *tua, Caesar, aetas* (Hor. 4, 15),
and he sings the praise of *imperi porrecta maiestas*, the majesty of the
empire that spread from the Eastern to the Western end of the
earth. Prophetically Virgil (*Aen.* I) made Iuppiter promise to the
son of Venus *imperium sine fine*, rule without limit. Sallust, Livy,
Valerius Maximus speak generally of the *imperium Romanum.*
Or in the inscription on the Cenotaph of C. Caesar in Pisa (*ILS* 140)
Augustus is called *custos imperi Romani totiusque orbis terrarum
praesesi*, not likely to be an official formula. We often find *Imperium
Romanum* replaced by *orbis terrarum* or *orbis Romanus.* I come back
to that in a few moments. It appears, for example, on the famous
monument of Narbo (*ILS* 112), where the day of Augustus' (i.e.
Octavian's) first *imperium*, a mere *imperium pro praetore*, is described
as *imperium orbis terrarum. Imperium* henceforth was chiefly connected with the Princeps. Remember the *lex de imperio Vespasiani*
(*ILS* 244). Apart from occasional variations, *imperium* now was
one of two things, either the dignity and absolute power of the
emperor or: the empire. The republican use of the various meanings
of the word never quite disappeared, and *imperium populi Romani*
remained a common phrase. Even *res publica* is still used, though
chiefly in retrospect of the Republic. But Ovid (*Trist.* 4, 4, 15)
could also call Augustus the *pater patriae*, the personified *res
publica.*

This seems the right moment to say a few words about monarchy
in Rome. The transition from early monarchy to the Republic has
been a subject of much recent research; I cannot go into what I feel
is largely a jungle of clever or less clever speculations; in particular
I do not believe in some of the equations drawn between the developments in Greece and Rome. The *regnum* of the legendary kings was
a historical period which left many important features to the
Republic; but it was not an object of political thought, apart from
the fact that it was deliberately banished from it. There was no
compromise between kingship and the *res publica.* Sulla and Caesar,

on the other hand, were more than anybody else the grave-diggers
of the Republic, although the former tried to revive the rule of the
senate, and the other anticipated the development of centuries to
come, in his attempt to combine *res publica* and a monarchical empire. Then came the Principate, the rule of the *princieps civium*.
But, as Tacitus (*Ann.* 1, 1) says of Augustus, 'under the name of
princeps he took everything under his *imperium*' (*cuncta . . . nomine
principis sub imperium accepit*). It was at the beginning neither pure
monarchy nor pure Republic, but though monarchy was soon
triumphant, it (i.e. Augustus in his *Res Gestae*) claimed to have
received its power from the people, it remained based on such
republican notions as the *auctoritas principis*, his *tribunicia potestas*,
and others. *Res publica* did not mean Republic, though for more
than a century some members of the old families were still hoping
for a revival of the Republic. It took time to change the old ruling
class into a new society, and thus change its outlook. A translation
of *res publica* by Commonwealth can perhaps be justified by the
fact that it was frequently used to stress the beneficial side of
monarchy. As Hadrian said, taking up the old slogan used by
Plautus (above p. 111): '*ita rem publicam gesturum ut sciret populi rem
esse, non propriam*'. A good princeps always acted *pro re publica*.
The mixture of loyalty and flattery, typical of the time, provided
a new slogan for the emperor: *bono rei publicae natus*, born for the
good of the *res publica*; it can be found from Augustus to the fourth
century. Deification points to the same. As Virgil (*ecl.* 1) says of
Augustus: '*namque erit ille mihi semper deus*' (he will always be a
god to me). The monarchy of the later centuries we call the Dominate. The word is a modern invention, in contrast to the Principate,
derived from the fact that the princeps had become *Dominus et
Deus*. This implies the gradual development from Roman and
largely republican forms through the increasing predominance of
purely military autocracy to the full impact of Hellenistic and
Oriental forms of kingship. In a sense, the programme of Caesar
had been carried out and completed. It is not surprising that the
words *rex* and – especially with Christian writers – *regnum* were
increasingly used. Ulpianus (*D.* 1, 4, 1 pr.) even calls the *lex de
imperio*, known to us from Vespasian onwards, a *lex regia*.

Some Roman concepts of state and empire

We return to the concepts of empire. Neither *res publica* nor *imperium* (with its twofold meaning) were suitable to describe it as a territorial unit as it had been seen through Roman eyes for a long time. The only really geographical term, which we have already met, is *orbis terrae* (or *orbis terrarum*). Our earliest evidence seems the passage already quoted from *Rhet. ad Herenn.* which belongs to the age of Sulla. Cicero in 63 (*pro Murena*, 22) praises military success as the safest basis for the consulship: *haec orbem terrarum parere huic imperio coegit.* There are many similar passages in Cicero. In a letter to Brutus (1, 16, 2) he even calls Caesar's murderers *liberatores orbis terrarum*. The *lex Gabinia Calpurnia* of 58 B.C., recovered for us in fragments at Delos (*SEG* I 335, 19), speaks of *imperio amplificato pace per orbem terrarum*: peace had extended the *imperium* all over the *orbis* which could be called *orbis Romanus*. Rome was the only ruling power, and her territory therefore identical with the whole world. A year later, Cicero quotes to Atticus (4, 1, 7) the words of the laws by which Pompey received power, among them the all-important on corn distribution, over the whole *orbis terrarum* (. . . *omnis potestas rei frumentariae toto orbe terrarum daretur*). The phrase became common in both official and unofficial use. *Orbis* was the sphere or globe, a symbol even in Hellenistic times of the world and of world rule. We find the picture of a globe on coins, usually with Roma or the *genius populi Romani*; a coin as early as c. 69 B.C. shows the goddess Roma with the globe and the figure of Italia with the *cornucopiae*, indicating the alliance after the Social War. Even more emphasis was laid on all this under and after Augustus, who used it in the first sentence of his *Res Gestae*, to describe how he subjected the *orbis terrarum* to the *imperium populi Romani*. The connection *urbs* and *orbis* appears in Varro (5, 143) who draws the etymological link between *urbs* and the *orbis* (circle) of the *pomerium*. In many *laudes Romae* from Livy to the late panegyrists, Rome is called time and again *caput orbis terrarum* or *lux orbis terrarum*. There was, after all, a state much larger than the *res publica*. The phrase *domina Roma*, first used by Horace (4, 14, 43), and in an anachronistic context about Scipio Africanus by Livy (38, 51, 4), was the verbal equivalent of the goddess with the globe. The fact of a real empire, not only of provinces ruled by Rome, was soon raised to an ideal level: it became the *orbis Romanus*, but never lost (as Joseph Vogt has shown) its universality. As the Greeks had spoken of the *oecumene*, thus the Roman *orbis terrarum* was identified with civilized mankind, and Greeks were among the first to identify the empire with the *orbis terrarum*. Roman rule was regarded as a stupendous achievement in creating unity, peace, prosperity. *Omnes gentes* were united in her empire. The most eloquent eulogist of Rome, Aelius Aristeides, identified the empire (*archē*) with the *oecumene* and praised the Romans for the generous grant of citizenship: 'You have caused the word Roman to be the label not of membership of a city, but of a common nationality' (if you will allow this translation of γένους ὄνομα κοινοῦ τινος). The walls of Rome, he says, are not around the city (this was in the second century, long before the Aurelian Wall), but at the frontiers of the empire.

Naturally enough, the emperors played their part in this game. They were called *orbis terrarum rector* or *pacator* or *custos*, later *restitutor* or *liberator*. In the fourth century we frequently read *toto orbe victor*, and with *dominus orbis* the world has become the emperor's own property; rather ironically this phrase was first used for Florianus, successor for only ninety days of the emperor Tacitus, though later for Gallienus, Diocletian, Julianus. On coins we find again the globe and legends such as *pax orbis*, *securitas orbis*, *gloria orbis*. Occasionally, places outside the Mediterranean area like Britain or Gades are regarded as Roman, but *extra orbem*. Thus, the equation with the whole known world did not always come true. The minimum and often the maximum extent included were the countries round the *mare nostrum*, with some continental areas in the North and East. In a half patriotic, half pedantic and technical way, one began to speak of the *orbis Romanus*, especially after the conflict with Germans and Persians became predominant. Finally the idea of a universal Roman empire prevailed. Most people, after the terrible conditions of the later third century, wanted nothing but peace and security, happier times (*felicia* or *feliciora tempora*). An amusing example of general feelings is provided by some game tablets, where six six-letter-words were needed. The general meaning is clear: after victory was won, *ludant Romani*! (let the Romans have their games!)[6] Through times better and worse, the unity of, and pride in, the empire were maintained, however threatened by barbarian inroads. These feelings were shared by pagans and Christians alike. The growing church took over what Rome had created. Tertullian called Christianity *gens totius orbis*, others write of the *una per omnem orbem terrae ecclesia diffusa*, the one church spread over the whole world. From Constantine onwards, *orbis* or *orbis Romanus* can mean the Christian world. St Augustine speaks of the *orbis catholicus* over against the heretics. Eventually, the Christian state, in most of its actions more state than Christian, achieved its sublime truth in the *Civitas Dei*.

Thus, at the end, as it were, of all the developments, stands St Augustine's contrasting couple of *civitas terrena* and *civitas Dei*. There can be little doubt that the essential background of the two *civitates* is the Christian exegesis of the Old Testament and its two cities of celestial Jerusalem and terrestrian Babylon. This is the fundamental explanation of Augustine's 'two kinds of human society' (*CD* 14, 1), based the one on *amor Dei*, the other on *amor sui* (14, 28), though the final separation of the two *civitates* will only occur *ultimo iudicio* (1, 35). The theologians are divided in their interpretations and the identity or non-identity of the *civitas Dei* with the *Ecclesia Christi*. This is not our concern. Augustine took a somewhat divided view of Roman history. He condemned the lust for power (*libido dominandi*), though he admired Roman patriotism and political organization. There were *civiles virtutes*, important even '*sine vera religione*', but the citizens were to be members of that *civitas* '*cuius rex veritas, cuius lex caritas, cuius modus aeternitas*' (*epist.* 138, 17), the community whose king is truth, whose law is charity, whose limit is eternity. In earlier centuries the standing of citizens had gradually declined, the contrast between *cives Romani* and *peregrini* had weakened. Eventually, all free members of the empire (with negligible exceptions) were made *cives* by the *Constitutio Antoniniana* of 212. Rome

[6] Tabulae lusoriae (see Pauly-Wissowa-Kroll *Real-Encyclopaedie f. d. klass. Altertumswissenschaft* XII, 2010 ff.) (third-fourth centuries A.D.

PARTHI OCCISI	VIRTUS IMPERI
BRITTO VICTUS	HOSTES VINCTI
LUDITE ROMANI	LUDANT ROMANI

had really become *communis patria* of all. Pride spread in what was now called *Romanitas*. A unified empire, based on Roman civilization, with thousands of barbarians especially in the army, had replaced a territory ruled by Roman citizens. To the church fathers, this unity and the *Pax Augusta* were necessary antecedents of Christ's empire.

Civitas, apart from being the original community of Roman citizens, had been for a long time any small community within the empire, not an abstract but like *populus* a body of men. However, since all men were *cives Romani*, *civitas* as citizenship was an expression of the unity of the empire, and thus of the empire itself. '*Regnum*' became fairly popular again, but as a neutral word, used both for the empire and the reign of Christ. Augustine followed earlier writers such as Tertullian who contrasted *Romani* or *cives* with *Christiani*, and regarded the whole empire as one *civitas*, personified in the *urbs*. *Res publica, urbs, civitas, imperium, regnum, orbis* (which all appear in Augustine) had grown into one, and by then, especially through Christian writers, outweighed all possible policy by individual emperors. *Urbs* and *orbis* with their similar sounds were identified. Augustine's mind was focused on the membership of either of his cities, on their *cives*. Thus, the word *civitas* (as *polis* with the Greek Christian writers) was a natural choice, although by then it meant state or empire rather than city. The *civitas terrena* was not simply Rome, but a kind of metaphysical contrast to the *civitas Dei*. Rome was in both.

8

❧✧❧

Caesar's final aims[1]

The murder of Caesar was an event which reverberated through the centuries, and judgments were greatly contrasted. Dante put Brutus and Cassius into the deepest circle of Hell. Machiavelli and the eighteenth century celebrated them as the great tyrannicides, the champions of liberty. Roman views contrasted equally.[2] At any rate, the event meant for Rome new chaos, new civil war. What does it mean to history? What I have said already shows that history has not finally judged. But the historian would very much like to know what would have happened if Caesar had not been killed at the age of fifty-six or fifty-seven. What were his plans for himself, for Rome, for the empire? We shall never know for certain; but in order to find out, or at least approach, the truth about Caesar, and at the same time to understand the conspirators, this is *the* crucial question. Many books and papers have been written on this question; ancient historians have

---

[1] © 1964 by the President and Fellows of Harvard College. This article was delivered as a lecture on 16 October 1962 at Harvard University on the invitation of its Department of Classics, and later published in the *Harvard Studies in Classical Philology*. My thanks are due to Mr R. A. G. Carson, Keeper of Coins in the British Museum, for the casts used for the plates of coins.
[2] Cf. the survey, and the attempt at an 'impartial' verdict, by W. Schmitt-henner *Geschichte in Wissenschaft und Unterricht* (1962), 685.

reason to be grateful to Brutus and Cassius for having substantially contributed to their livelihood.

Nobody doubts that Caesar had a quasi-monarchical position when he died. The question really is whether he was satisfied with that or wanted more. There is also the additional question in what ways his position was expressed. The answers to these questions are made difficult chiefly by the fact that most of our evidence is of later date, when Caesar had become *Divus Iulius* to be followed by other *Divi* and emperors whose positions approached or reached that of the *Dominus et Deus*. After Mommsen's idealization of the great statesman as an almost messianic figure had lost its immediate impact, though not its brilliance, modern views can be divided into two extreme and contradictory beliefs; either Caesar held the Roman, and, as it were, republican, autocracy of an *imperator* by way of a permanent dictatorship, or his was to be a divine kingdom (*deus et rex*), following the Hellenistic pattern. It is surprising to find that the division among scholars is largely along national lines. Most German and French historians believe in the 'God and King' – even Professor Gelzer, who is fully aware of the clever politician Caesar;[3] most British scholars deny the divinity as well as the kingship. American scholars such as Professor Lily Ross Taylor[4] and Mr Collins[5] are inclined to accept the position most decidedly expressed by Eduard Meyer,[6] while the British point of view has recently been restated by Mr Balsdon[7] and Mr Carson.[8] In a category of his own is Professor

[3] M. Gelzer *Caesar. Der Politiker und Staatsmann* (1960). I ought to add, however, that E. Badian in his review of Gelzer's book (*Gnomon*, 1961, 597) discovers 'two Caesars . . . dwelling in his breast', the practical politician as well as the superman of Mommsen's stamp. To a certain degree, Gelzer, as his title indicates, would probably agree with this description.

[4] Lily Ross Taylor *The Divinity of the Roman Emperor* (1931), 60, and *Party Politics in the Age of Caesar* (1949), 174.

[5] John H. Collins *Historia* IV (1955), 445.

[6] Eduard Meyer *Caesars Monarchie und das Principat des Pompeius* (1922), *passim*.

[7] J. P. V. D. Balsdon *Historia* VII (1958), 80, an article written with the author's usual acumen and wit, but not quite convincing.

[8] R. A. G. Carson *Gnomon* (1956), 181 (review of Alföldi and Kraft – see notes 9 and 15). [Helga Gesche *Die Vergottung Caesars* (Frankf. Althist. Studien) Heft. 1 (1968) denies any deification in Caesar's lifetime.]

Alföldi,[9] who not only suggested a new chronology of the last two months of Caesar's life, but also argues that Caesar aimed at a renewal of the ancient Roman kingdom. Let me say at once that such labels as Hellenistic or Roman kingship, though they may sometimes be necessary, are not without danger. They may cover too much or too little; they can even distort the facts. I shall try to get down to the facts as far as we know them.

A few more remarks about our sources – at least the literary ones – without which even the coins remain in a vacuum, eloquent but ambiguous: the most important are of course the contemporary ones, that is, Cicero and his correspondents. There are a few relevant passages in Cicero, and, as Sir Frank Adcock says,[10] 'their fewness should teach us to be on our guard'. That is certainly right, but at the same time they do say a great deal, and in view of this it remains astonishing that modern scholars disagree to such an extent. There is, however, universal agreement that Suetonius and Dio have preserved some first-class material, partly authentic utterances, partly evidence from the *acta senatus*. Mr Balsdon, who warns us against using these sources, nevertheless does use them on several occasions without any additional evidence. One possible trap for the historian is that he may confuse senatorial decrees in Caesar's honour, proposed by his followers or by opponents acting as '*agents provocateurs*', with honours which Caesar himself either accepted or assumed; another is that he may follow the principle of *quod non est in actis non est in vita*. To give one example: on 17 March the senate made the famous self-contradictory decision to abolish dictatorship and to confirm all of Caesar's *acta*; none of his decrees was revoked. Balsdon thinks this decree shows that Caesar had done nothing to set himself up as a god and king. But does it? We shall see that the evidence on this issue

---

[9] Andreas Alföldi *Studien über Caesars Monarchie* (1953); cf. *Schweizer Münz-blätter* (1953), Heft 13. Professor Alföldi tells me that he is preparing a new work, based on a vast amount of numismatic evidence. Naturally, this will be expected with the greatest interest. So far, his theories have found little acclamation. Cf., e.g., R.A.G. Carson *Greece and Rome* (1957), 46. D. Felber in: F. Altheim and D. Felber *Einzeluntersuchungen zur altitalischen Geschichte* (1961), 211.

[10] F. E. Adcock *Cambridge Anc. Hist.* IX (1932), 718.

simply could not be in the *acta*. Anyway, certain facts emerge from the contemporary sources, and we are justified in using at least some of the later corroborative material.

Something can be learned from Caesar's verdict on Sulla. In March 49, Caesar wrote to Oppius, his well-known political agent, with the intention that the letter should be shown to Cicero (*Att.* IX 7 C), that he did not aim at imitating Sulla, who was the only one to keep the fruits of victory for any length of time; what was to distinguish Caesar from Sulla was *misericordia et liberalitas*, in short the famous *clementia*. No proscriptions for him.

This was not merely propaganda; Caesar stuck to the principle to the end. What otherwise? Suetonius (77) has preserved Caesar's own words describing Sulla as an illiterate in politics, and the *res publica* as a mere name without substance. Sulla had been *dictator rei publicae constituendae* and had eventually resigned, leaving the restored *res publica* under the senate's weak leadership and at the mercy of political generals such as Pompey. Caesar, whose dictatorship, at least since Thapsus (46 B.C.), was perhaps *rei publicae constituendae*, made this title meaningless by becoming dictator first for ten years and then *in perpetuum*, the latter (according to the traditional chronology) before the Lupercalia of 44. Caesar thus destroyed the very nature of the *dictatura*, the time limit which was the republican safeguard against one man's supreme power. Caesar started his dictatorships by trying to stick to constitutional legality, but that went overboard with the third and fourth dictatorships in 46 and 45. At the same moment when Caesar brought an ancient Roman tradition of extraordinary office to a culmination, its very nature as an office was destroyed. In a different sense he proved again that he was not a second Sulla, no illiterate in politics, not concerned with maintaining the empty form of the *res publica*.

Now Cicero. The relations between the two are in general well-known facts of history. What we want to see is the impact of the man Caesar, and of his position in his last years, on such an impressionable mind as Cicero's. In May 45, Cicero wrote to Atticus (XII 40) of his futile attempts to compose a *Symbouleutikos*, a book of theoretical advice and philosophical interpretation of a ruler's duties, after the examples set by Aristotle and by Theopompus, who wrote *Ad*

Alexandrum. He cannot, as they did, write *honesta et grata Alexandro.* 'Sed quid simile?' A fortnight later he makes it quite clear why the ruler Caesar was not an object for advisory approach. In the meantime Caesar had become *synnaos Quirini* (XII 45), and the intended new *domus regia* was to be the neighbour of Atticus on the Quirinalis. With bitter sarcasm Cicero writes that he prefers Caesar's statue with Quirinus rather than with Salus; with the deified Romulus, who according to one legend was murdered by senators, rather than with the deity of health and prosperity. Caesar belonged, in Cicero's view, to the same class as Alexander or Romulus, though he was much worse than either. Caesar's statue in the temple may not have implied divinity for him, nor Cleopatra's for her in the temple of Venus Genetrix, the goddess of the Iulian house; but both were certainly raised high above human level. For such a sober historian as Gelzer (and others) these facts are the confirmation of established ruler worship. Caesar was *parens patriae*, the originator, if only the re-originator, of the state, as had been Romulus, the first and the only deified king of Rome. Alexander, Cicero writes, did not become proud, cruel, and immoderate *postquam rex appellatus est.* How different with Caesar! How could he, after his *pompa* as the *contubernalis Quirini* have any pleasure in Cicero's moderate *epistulae*? Clearly, to Cicero, then, Caesar was in a position not essentially different from that of a king. This is not refuted by the fact that, when Cicero spoke for the king Deiotarus in the presence of Caesar and mentioned some slander against the latter because of the *statua inter reges posita*, he added with some irony: *nam de statua quis queritur, una praesertim, cum tam multas videat?* Moreover, the solemn procession in which Caesar's statue was carried to the temple gave him at least the appearance of a divine person.

Some scholars have argued that these facts do not provide any proof of a divine role because Augustus likewise accepted some of these honours, for example, the connection with Romulus-Quirinus and statues in various temples. Events one or two generations later do not necessarily mean the same as did earlier ones. In any case, Augustus by his very name had become more than an ordinary mortal, and though he restricted some attempts at giving him divine honours, there is evidence to show that even in the West he could be called a god. Comparisons between Caesar and Augustus are natural, and can be illuminating either way, from Caesar to Augustus or vice versa, but they can never give absolute certainty.

Things came even more into the open in July 45 when in the *pompa* of the *ludi Victoriae Caesaris* his statue was carried alongside and together with those of Victoria and other gods. When Brutus tried to persuade Cicero to come into Caesar's presence, he replied: *pompa deterret*. He sometimes calls Caesar *rex*. It is true that *regnum* and *regnare*, even *rex*, are general words and do not mean much, especially when they are used in an informal way of bitter half-joking resignation. 'I know that he is a king, but there is no fight left in me' (*Att.* 13, 37). After the Ides of March Cicero writes to Matius, one of the most decent and selfless among Caesar's followers: *si Caesar rex fuerit – quod mihi quidem videtur* (*fam.* 11, 27). To others, at that time, he speaks only of the *tyrannos*.

No doubt Cicero's own attitude wavered. He declared *non omnibus servire* ('I do not wish to attend to Caesar's creatures'), and yet he sometimes was keen enough not to lose contact. We have the famous letter in which he describes Caesar's visit to him in December 45 (*Att.* 13, 52): '*homines visi sumus* – we were quite human together. Still, you would not say to Caesar: *amabo te*, I shall be your friend, come back to my house on your return journey. Oh no: *semel satis est.*' Caesar himself realized that his treatment of men like Cicero, who had to wait in the antechamber for an audience, was bound to make enemies (*Att.* 14, 1). Cicero detested the whole corrupt court atmosphere of Caesar's surroundings (cf. *fam.* 6, 19, 2), though even in that he was not quite consistent. Well known are his bitter jokes about the degradation of the highest republican office when Caesar appointed a consul for the last few hours of the year, the consul under whom nobody ever had lunch and no crime was committed, and who never even slept during his whole consulship. Funny, isn't it? Yes, but: *quae si videres lacrimas non teneres.*

We may think that none of the passages in Cicero's letters clearly says that Caesar was a deified king. But it is equally true that we cannot deny the fact that there was a great deal in his position that was at variance with Roman republican traditions. The decisive point in my view is that the facts, though not the constitutional forms and names, gave Caesar a status far above a mere dictatorship, even one for life. As Cicero puts it when he speaks of Antony having abolished the *dictatura* (*Phil.* I 3): *quae iam vim regiae potestatis obsederat* – 'which had already gained the strength of royal power'. It is also significant both for Cicero and for Caesar that in 45 the orator in his speech *pro rege Deiotaro*, facing Caesar and speaking in Caesar's house, the *regia* of the *pontifex maximus*, enumerated the *regiae laudes*: to be brave, just, severe, magnaminous, bountiful, beneficent, noble. He even maintained that *semper regium nomen in hac civitate sanctum fuit*, though that of the *reges socii et amici* was *sanctissimum*. Naturally, all this did not refer to a Roman king, but it shows a willingness (certainly not quite genuine and perhaps even with a touch of irony) to recognize the value of monarchy and the ideal of Greek monarchical theory. Caesar was a *rex*, though not by name, and we do realize that the nomenclature is by no means unimportant. It would not be good enough just to say: what's in a name anyway?

What about the god Caesar? The two decisive passages are *Philippics* II 110 (repeated in the following paragraph) and XIII 41. 47 (cf. Suet. *Caes.* 76). The former is called by Sir Ronald Syme (who agrees on this point with Sir Frank Adcock) 'a difficult passage',[11] and in a note of two lines he adds: 'It can hardly be proved that Caesar devised a comprehensive policy of ruler-worship.' That is begging the question. Professor Vogt[12] has said essential things about the passage: *quem in honorem maiorem consecutus erat* (what higher honours had he reached) *quam uti haberet pulvinar, simulacrum, fastigium, flaminem*? We discuss the four concepts. The *pulvinar* was a couch made of cushions, used in the *lectisternium*, a ritual feast of the gods whose statues or symbols were lying on those cushions and who were given a banquet (actually later eaten by the *epulones*). A special *lectisternium* on a special day was given in honour of Caesar. He must have been among the gods of the state. A *simulacrum* was a statue, normally that of a god to be worshipped. We remember Caesar's statue in the temple of Quirinus, and also the one carried in a *pompa*

[11] R. Syme *The Roman Revolution* (1939), 54, 4.
[12] Joseph Vogt 'Zum Herrscherkult bei Julius Caesar' *Studies Presented to David M. Robinson* II (1953), 1138.

circensis at least on two occasions, always in the company of gods. A *fastigium* was a gable, pediment, usually, though not necessarily, of a sacred building. It may have meant the *regia* of the *pontifex maximus*, and thus Caesar's house. Calpurnia, on the night before the Ides of March, saw the pediment of Caesar's house crashing down, and understandably took it as a sign of danger. A coin of 44 (Sydenham 1076) shows a temple front, with a globe in the *tympanum fastigii*, the inner triangle of the gable. In any case, in the context in Cicero, the pediment must have had some connection with the worship of Caesar. Finally *flamen*: Cicero (II 110) continues: *est ergo flamen ut Iovi, ut Marti, ut Quirino, sic divo Iulio M. Antonius?* In XIII, Cicero repeats that Antony was Caesar's *flamen*, although after the murder he did not act as such. *Cuius flaminium cur reliquisti?* The answer is, of course, that an official divine worship of Caesar was impossible in the days after his death. Balsdon says[13] that there had been no initiation of Antony to the office; but that would have happened only if Caesar had not been killed. Otherwise, Cicero's remarks would be completely senseless. Antony also avoided all reference to a deified Caesar in his speeches; he calls him *tantus vir* or *clarissimus civis*; but then he was in fear for his own life.

I am convinced that Cicero spoke as he did because he wanted to describe Caesar as a god. Here we may be entitled to consider some later evidence. Dio and even Plutarch confirm Cicero's account. Dio (43, 45, 3) tells us that the statue in the temple of Quirinus had the inscription *deo invicto*, and that Caesar's statue was carried in the *pompa* with those of the other gods. So far he only confirms Cicero. When he adds that Caesar's statue was to be erected in all cities and in all temples in Rome, this will probably be an exaggeration; but there were so many unusual and, in fact, immoderate honours showered on Caesar – all decreed by the senate in 45 and 44, all accepted by Caesar, and all in the line of either royal or super-human qualities – that Antony could reproach Cicero by saying it had been done in order to give a false picture of Caesar and to rouse misgivings (Cic. *Phil.* XIII). That, of course, was at a time when Antony endeavoured to minimize the facts which were the decisive

---

[13] Balsdon (above, n. 7), 84.

Caesar's final aims

causes of the conspiracy. As Cicero says: *tu, tu illum occidisti Lupercalibus.*

The famous scene to which Cicero refers is described in greater detail in *Philippics* II and elsewhere; it is known from many sources. 'What is more shameful than the fact that that man is alive who would have placed the diadem on Caesar's head, while the man who refused it was, as everybody agrees, justly slain?' Caesar ordered the following to be written in the *fasti* on the occasion of the Lupercalia: *C. Caesari, dictatori perpetuo, M. Antonium consulem populi iussu regnum detulisse. Caesarem uti noluisse.* This asks for some comment. *Regnum*: clearly, here kingdom and cult meet again; the diadem which Caesar had refused was hung in the temple of Iuppiter, the only accepted king of Rome. But was it offered *populi iussu*? No *comitia* had decided on this, nor had the consul acted on the senate's advice. S.P.Q.R. had no say in this, and we know from Cicero how little the people responded to the name of *rex*, how definitely they had applauded Caesar's refusal. Even the wording of the inscription seems to show that Caesar refused under public pressure.

Caesar dedicated the diadem to Iuppiter Capitolinus. This fact has been given a new aspect by the discovery of a unique coin by Professor Alföldi[14] – *if* the coin is genuine and its interpretation accepted (see Plate Ia). CAESAR DICT. QUART.; mintmaster Mettius, i.e. early 44. In many coins of the same type we have the *lituus*, the augur's staff, the other way round (Plate Ib); in that case no alteration of an existing coin into the diadem was possible. Alföldi believes that the one isolated coin pictures the diadem hung up in the temple. If so, it would mean that this particular coin was issued immediately after the Ides of February, the date of the Lupercalia, and that DICT. PERP. thus dates even later than that. Strong doubts have been expressed about the whole argument. It is a matter for the numismatists to decide; but the outsider cannot suppress his doubts whether in an official issue the 'I' in DICT could be deleted by the symbol depicted. As far as I know, nothing similar ever happens on coins of the period. There were issues with the *lituus* the other way round (Plate Ic), but not with Mettius as the mintmaster. Coins of 63 B.C. with

---

[14] For Alföldi, see above, n. 9.

135

the head of the king Ancus Marcius (Plate Id), looking like Caesar's elder brother, show the royal diadem, a clear anachronism under Hellenistic influence. The diadem must have been in late Republican times a somewhat natural symbol of kingship. Caesar refused it – what did he wear? We all know: a laurel wreath. But if one looks at most of Caesar's coins (Plates Ic, IIg), one sees a wreath of a very peculiar kind. This is a discovery by Professor Kraft.[15] Incidentally, the coin in Plate Id shows the kind of *lituus* which could easily be turned into Alföldi's diadem. As to the wreath, we need only compare, for example, an Augustus coin (Plate Ie): twigs with natural leaves, sometimes fruits, bound together in the back with a bow. Caesar's wreath, on the other hand, is a stylized affair, closely fitted, less broad, and without any tie in the back, but protruding over the forehead. In this form it even survived in coins after his death (Plate IIf). It looks like metal work and since we know that Caesar wore a golden wreath the whole thing is clear enough; it is most surprising that for generations no one, whether numismatist or not, had noticed the difference; people only varied in calling it either a laurel wreath or a diadem. It is neither, and Kraft has shown analogies in Etruscan pictures. The triumphal costume which, we are told, Caesar normally wore in public, the purple toga, is also attributed to Etruscan origin. This was most probably the costume of the Etruscan kings, while the red shoes which also belong to Caesar's dress are supposed to derive from the early kings of Alba Longa. But it does not follow from these facts (as Kraft assumes) that this costume, including the golden wreath, was the dress of the old Roman kings. It may be assumed *a priori* to be unlikely, since the last Etruscan king in Rome was the hated representative of tyranny, quite apart from the general feelings about a Roman *rex*. We can be certain only that the Etruscan fashion of a festive golden crown was accepted by Caesar; he wore it even with the veil of the *pontifex maximus*.

What meaning do these facts have with respect to Caesar's position in the last period of his life? Worship and divinity seem to me beyond any reasonable doubt. Caesar's power and his honours were

---

[15] K. Kraft 'Der goldene Kranz Caesars' *Jahrbuch für Numismatik und Geldgeschichte 1952/3* (1955).

Plate I Casts of coins in the British Museum (magnification 2:1)

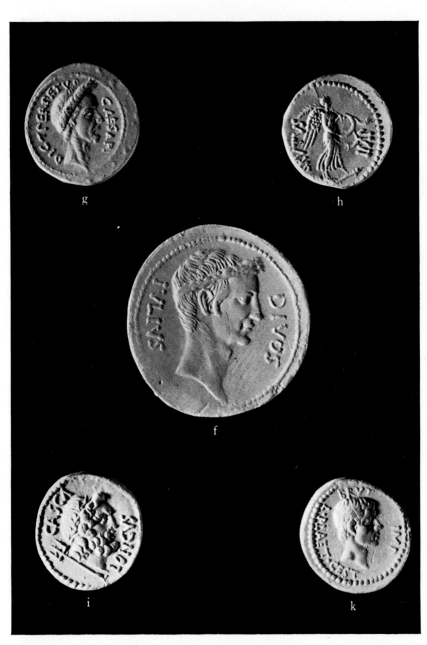

g

h

f

i

k

Plate II   Casts of coins of Caesar and Brutus in the British Museum (magnification 2:1)

limitless, though not regal by title. Much was mere flattery and servility on the part of the senate; but Caesar could have refused if he wanted (as he did refuse a few honours, however reluctantly), and others were clearly *acta Caesaris*, or *acta senatus*, above all his *flamen* and most of the things mentioned by Cicero in *Philippics* II. Among the actual happenings, for example, were that the month Quintilis became Iulius, that the fifth day of the *ludi Romani* was dedicated to Caesar, that oaths were taken by his *genius*, the divine spirit living in Caesar, that he had in the senate an elevated golden seat, a real throne, that he was *praefectus morum* and – like Romulus – *parens patriae*. We need not add all the rumours and ideas which went even beyond what has been mentioned, among them, Dio's story that Caesar was to be buried, again like Romulus, inside the *pomerium*. Adcock says:[16] 'Caesar was killed because of what he was, not because of what he might be.' That sounds convincing, though I doubt whether those *imponderabilia* could not be weighty facts; the conspirators would hardly make a fine distinction between facts and possibilities when the possibilities included all their fears. In any event, they found enough reasons even to convince Brutus, and we can still recognize them.

One thing seems to speak against us. Did Caesar ever attempt to create a dynasty? His adoption of the young Octavius, whom by testament he made his private heir, does not mean that he saw in the boy of eighteen his successor as the ruler of Rome. Octavian, as we call him, knew nothing of Caesar's last will, though I do not accept the theory that the whole adoption was a later political manoeuvre by Octavian.[17] It is surprising, on the other hand, to find that even such a great and realistic historian as Rostovtzeff[18] took the adoption as 'clear proof that Caesar regarded Octavian as his heir and inheritor of his position'. There was nobody else however – certainly not Marc Antony – whom he might choose. He wanted a son, and in his last will provided for a possible posthumous son by Calpurnia.

[16] Adcock (above, n. 10), 724.
[17] W. Schmitthenner 'Oktavian und das Testament Caesars' *Zetemata*, Heft 4 (1952). Even though I cannot quite accept Schmitthenner's conclusions, this is a most valuable and interesting thesis.
[18] M. Rostovtzeff *History of the Ancient World* II (1927), 147.

Cleopatra never had a decisive influence on Caesar; but was she the mother of his son? When she was in Rome in 45–44, she must have been in an advanced state of pregnancy; it would be curious if Caesar did not mind, unless the child born soon afterward, the unhappy Caesarion, was really his son (a fact denied by Balsdon). Anyway, he could never regard him as a possible successor. Caesar, at the age of fifty-seven, though not very healthy and quite aware of the danger of a conspiracy, did not think that his life was at its end. The stories about his playing with the idea of death look very much like tales told after the event. We may search for various psychological reasons; we may think that his intended form of rule was entirely personal – at any rate, he made no attempt to arrange for his succession.

Does that mean that he did not wish to be a king? Some scholars are too much inclined to assume that Caesar's monarchy, practically established except in name, must have been a copy of the Hellenistic type, *basileus* instead of *rex*. The decadent and powerless kings of the time, in spite of Cleopatra, did not provide very worthy models. Neither were Caesar's aims simply in the Roman tradition. How indeed could they be? Syme's statement[19] that Caesar was a truer Roman than either Pompey or Augustus seems to me incomprehensible – unless Rome and greatness are regarded as identical. The absolute break with that tradition is all too obvious. Can we not assume, in fact must we not do so, that Caesar intended to create his own form of monarchy – neither Roman nor Hellenistic but Caesarean? He took from various traditions whatever symbols he found suitable, what circumstances seemed to demand, what might make a compromise possible. Moreover, Caesar may not yet have shaped the ultimate form of his monarchy and thus have added to our difficulties. At all events, he did not leave it ready and finished for a possible successor.

There are other features to support our view. The *pompa*, for instance, which made such a devastating impression on Cicero, was clearly in the Roman tradition, a form of divine worship long practised in Rome. Clearly, too, it was connected with the *pompa trium-*

[19] Syme (above, n. 11), 54.

phalis – nothing more Roman than that, whatever its origins. But Caesar's statue appeared next to that of Victoria, and we cannot help remembering that famous procession in which, at a Dionysiac festival, the second Ptolemy celebrated his ancestors, and Alexander and Ptolemy I appeared in the company of deities and divine personifications. Surely in Caesar's *pompa* different elements were combined. Or the globe which appears on some of Caesar's coins, as in fact it had already, since the seventies, in connection with the *genius populi Romani* or the *dea Roma*; now we are told (Dio 43. 14, 6; 21, 2) of a statue of Caesar with his feet on a globe; we remember that Demetrius Poliorcetes, the very personification of Hellenistic divine kingship, was represented the same way. More significantly still, Caesar was also the first Roman to put his own portrait on coins, as had been usual with Alexander and many Hellenistic kings, thus taking a place normally filled by a deity. If, politically, Caesar's position had not completely outgrown Roman dictatorship (though very little thereof was left), the religious side of his position was, to say the least, strongly influenced by Hellenistic ideas and institutions. From both these sources and, as we now know, from an Etruscan tradition as well, came the streams which joined in one concept, still growing, not yet completed, but there for everyone to see, the shape of Caesar's monarchy. He had his court and his ministers; Cicero complains of both more than once. In Caesar's own vision, politics and religion, Roman and non-Roman features, were one as the expression of his rulership.

The picture which we have in our minds of the last months of Caesar's life is shaped and overshadowed by our knowledge of what was to be the end. If I have concentrated on his personal position, this is, I believe, justifiable; in fact, it is the clue to almost everything. What he did and planned for Rome and the empire largely depended on his own power and authority. Still, in talking about Caesar's final aims we must not forget the solid work that he was doing for the pacification of the empire and for the necessary, if dangerous, transformation of Roman society. In 46, in his speech *pro Marcello*, Cicero had urged Caesar to dedicate himself, after his many great military actions, to the work of peaceful reconstruction. No doubt Caesar did carry out a programme of political and social planning that was more urgent than anything else. But he also prepared for a war against Parthia and Dacia. Was that equally urgent? Ever since Carrhae, Parthia constituted a threat to the province of Syria, as was later confirmed by Antony's campaigns. There was also a widespread desire in Rome to take vengeance for Crassus' defeat and to display Roman strength in the East; that was ultimately confirmed by the emphasis laid on Augustus' peaceful but dignified settlement in 20 B.C. Further, in the Northeast a Dacian realm had arisen, and the lasting threat to that frontier was intensified. Caesar acted as the great soldier and empire-builder he was when he decided on war; he may have thought that victory would solve other problems as well. Once again he would be acclaimed as *imperator*, the title prominent on his coins during those months, and thus receive a new sanction from the Roman people, who had just shown their dislike of the royal diadem.

I have mentioned Cicero's reactions; but he was not one of the conspirators, although his name was their catchword after the event: *Cicero et libertas!* The reaction of Brutus and Cassius is reflected in their coins. There is the famous one with the Phrygian cap and two daggers, and the legends either EID MAR or LIBERTAS. *Libertas* was a concept which could be understood in very different ways; we must not build on that word. But there is another coin of BRUTUS IMP; on its reverse we see (Plate IIh) Victoria with an ear of corn, symbolizing peace and prosperity, tearing up a diadem and treading on a broken sceptre, the two outstanding symbols of kingship. The sceptre had appeared on most of Caesar's Eastern coins; in Rome it had been a symbol only of deified Rome. It is obvious what feelings the conspirators had about Caesar's position. The coins, although *post eventum* and certainly propaganda, are nevertheless significant. After all, Brutus was the one man whose prestige made the conspiracy really possible, and not only because in the summer or autumn of 45 he had married Cato's daughter. He probably married her – against the wish of his mother, Caesar's former mistress – because of his innate 'Catonism'. The conspiracy was directed against the enemy of the Republic, the monarch Caesar. And yet, the same coins of Brutus showed on the obverse the head either of Neptune or of Brutus himself (Plate IIi, IIk). Is it a sign of the weakness in the republican traditions that their champion followed Caesar's unique precedent?

Caesar had accepted certain symbols of divine rulership. He had also turned the *insignia* and the dress of the triumphator into distinctive features of his appearance. He could not intend eternally to celebrate a triumph – rather they became the outward signs of his kingship. If he did use some *insignia* of Etruscan kingship, he did so not to renew that obsolete institution, but to find new symbols for his own monarchy. He was the *unus imperator in toto imperio* (Cic. *pro Lig.* 5), the *invictus* who was more than even a *dictator perpetuus*. The story of the Sibylline oracle which pronounced that only a king would conquer the Parthians may have been an invention or a mere rumour, though it may have been true that Caesar declared that he was not a king in Rome or Italy, but would go out to the war as the king of the provinces. Anyway, Caesar was the commander of all armed forces whatever they were; he was the real ruler of the empire, of the *orbis Romanus*. In an empire only recently delivered from internecine war, the head of the army was the head of the empire. The city-state of Rome, even in its extension over Italy, had shown itself incapable of ruling an empire. New forms of government had to be found. A beginning was made by Caesar's policy of founding colonies all over the empire and extending Roman citizenship on a generous scale. After having firmly established (or so he believed) the unity of Italy up to the Alps, he had begun to weld the empire together on a new basis. This does not mean that he no longer regarded Rome and Italy as the centre, or that he was to become an Oriental sultan. The rumours about his intention to create a new capital in Alexandria or in Ilium, or that he intended to have several wives in order to be sure of begetting a son, were mere rumours and cannot be believed. Caesar did not imitate the Hellenistic divine kings, not even Alexander, but he did go far beyond the framework of Roman traditions. He had the vision of a united empire under the rule of Rome, and of a mixture of Italic and Greek populations. He tried – with the true insight of a genius and with equal carelessness for his own fate – to anticipate the development of the next two or three centuries. He may have shown in his last year a few signs of megalomaniac decline; but even if that were true, it was not the real

Caesar. A deified ruler, not a Hellenistic or Roman king, but an imperial one – that was most likely his final aim. We reach the conclusion that Caesar approached a form of rule which was to materialize much later, in which Roman and Hellenistic elements were joined by Oriental features, and shaped into something new. He was to be the ruler of an empire, the first Roman emperor.

9

Remarks on the meaning of history[1]

I. AIMS AND LIMITS

In the following pages I shall try to discuss some of the fundamental problems with which every thinking historian must wrestle now and then. We are told,[2] admittedly, that 'British historians are not very ready to give an answer' to what is described as a request, made by the reading public, 'for a final interpretation of history' or 'the question why civilizations rise and fall'. I fully understand this reluctance which is, at least in part, an outcome of some of the best qualities of British historical scholarship, its realism, its soundness, its honesty. But does it necessarily follow that 'the answers which are given are not put forward by the most learned or the most profound scholars'? I simply cannot believe that this is a fair statement. Is it a token of learnedness or profundity to be able to split one's own mind so that a person may have certain beliefs and convictions of which he or she as a historian need take no notice? At the risk of being either classified among those historians of minor rank or accused of importing some foreign product, I propose to discuss a few of the fundamental

[1] Written in its original form in 1944, with a number of later corrections and additions.
[2] By E. L. Woodward in his excellent survey of *British Historians* (1943), 48. All the quotations in this paragraph are from that page.

questions and thus to approach, if possible, 'a more definite judgement upon the pattern of history and the meaning of human existence'.

I spoke of trying to discuss some fundamental problems. I fear this sounds much too ambitious for what I am going to attempt. I admit that I am relying rather strongly on the goodwill and the generosity of my readers in inviting them to the following incomplete and aphoristic remarks. My excuse is the hope that others will take up the discussion. Historians are usually shy of learned volumes about the philosophy of history. The fact that I do not belong to any school of philosophy and, in fact, would not dare to call my thoughts philosophical, may perhaps induce one historian or another to publish some of his views on the meaning of history. The philosophers will call us amateurs, *dilettanti*. By all means. I for my part do not mind being called a 'lover' of that great lady Clio.

My answer to the question of what is the pattern, the purpose, the real meaning, of history will of necessity be fragmentary and incomplete. It will also be subjective. But so will every other answer, however comprehensive. There is no need to apologize. As far as we can think ahead, there is no one way for everybody, and there will be no one way – probably for a long time to come. Living through history, suffering by history, glorying in history, this generation of ours will hardly reach a common understanding of history. The obvious meaning of the war against criminal *hubris* and mad cruelty, a war, in fact, of Man against Leviathan, is contradicted by the equally obvious meaninglessness of the suffering of millions of innocent people. I shall not try to give a rational explanation for a discrepancy which ultimately can be overcome by personal faith alone. But at a moment when our very civilization seems on the verge of destruction, we naturally ask why things have come to this point, and whether there is some meaning in the general ruin. Has man completely lost his way? Can the past explain the present, and perhaps even give some hope for the future? In putting such or similar questions we may find that we are no longer satisfied with answers which were given in times – fairly recent times, in fact – when the world looked more or less safe and comfortable. Our world has changed, and many of the things which formerly seemed important or were fashionable have ceased to be of interest and significance. On the other hand, anything of lasting relevance has come, or will come, into its own again. In the bewilderment of these years we listen more eagerly than ever to every genuine and sincere voice, but we have become sceptical of others who promised more than they could fulfil. Everybody must try to find firm ground again. And the historian – can anybody blame him for this? – will turn to history.

He has, however, to realize that he is by no means the only, not even the main, interpreter of the pattern of history. There are others who have to say much of importance, the theologian and the philosopher for example, who always were the first to put questions and to give answers. Now there are also the scientist and the sociologist, the very representatives of our own age. It is only natural for the historian to feel humble in such company; but since the question with which we are concerned cannot be answered without some knowledge of history, he has to stand his ground, however diffident he may feel.

Let us start from facts. In other words, let us give a first chance to the historian and the scientist. The others will not be kept out for long. Both the historian and the scientist (and, I believe, the theologian and the sociologist as well), if they honestly try to get to the bottom of their subjects, must eventually face the problem of the origin of man. To put a large and intricate problem in the form of a simple alternative we can say: is the origin of man ultimately explained by pure evolution or by creation?

As the matter stands, at least as far as I know (and I must admit that my knowledge is very limited), no evolutionist up to now, in trying to show that evolution without creation is possible, has shown that creation is impossible. Moreover, various kinds of scientists have been very busy describing the conditions of the origin of human life, and in fact of organic life in general. Their theories lead us back for more than a thousand million years, and to the most primitive microorganisms. But all the wonderful discoveries of science cannot prove, I believe, that a purely automatic chemical process took the place of a *prima causa*, of spontaneous creation. Whether life can emerge from dead matter, as some scientists maintain, or not, the non-scientist, I believe, has the right to accept the view that organic life was 'created'. And then there is no reason not to assume that the same happened with inorganic matter.[3] If the world was created, and man in it (however small his place may have been, and still may be), it is hard to believe that the creative force for many millennia had nothing to do with the development of that created world; in the history of life and the history of man we ought to be able to trace some meaning connected with that creative force we call God, however different our conceptions of God may be. It is, of course, possible that our intellect, our imagination, our spiritual forces in general, are much too feeble to do the tracing of which I spoke. But the attempt must be made, as it has been made again and again throughout the ages. For our quest for the meaning of history will remain totally irrelevant, unless we try to give some answer, however incomplete, to the question of what is, or at least what may be, the part of God in human history.

2. THE HISTORIAN'S TASK

Before we try to get onto the road which leads to this last and greatest question, I should like to explore a sort of footpath which, I hope, will bring us nearer to the ultimate goal, even though it may be a detour. I wish to say something more of the meaning of *writing* and *studying* history, which is – and not only through the ambiguity of the word 'history' in English, which can mean the events of the past or the writing about them, i.e. historiography – a real and essential part of the wider and deeper question. For history as the total of past human experience can have no meaning for the present and future unless its facts are understood and studied, discussed and written down. Every new generation has a new and different understanding of, and relation to, the past, while at the same time the past, as it were, changes its appearance, recent events being added, earlier seen in a new light, others dropped into the darkness of oblivion. That aspect of history as something always renewed, reconsidered, re-

[3] [This is the 'Creation from Nothing' of Mysticism. Cf. G. Scholem *Eranos-Jahrbuch 1956* (25, 1957), 87 ff.]

written, the process which G. R. Elton calls 'the Practice of History', is in itself proof of its being alive and full of meaning. There is a vital urgency for every present to be in close contact with every past.

Therefore, if we can reach an understanding of to what end we study and write history we shall have gone a long way towards the final goal of understanding the meaning of history itself. The natural point of view for any attempt of this kind seems to be that of universal history, but we at once realize that the historical individuality of any nation, region, personality, or what else, has also something to do with the general meaning. Time and again the task is to bridge the gulf between universal and particular history, to see them in their mutual connections, and to learn what they have to tell us. This sounds fairly simple, but it is not. It is so difficult, not to say impossible, that we shall have to content ourselves with a compromise of one sort or another. The task is, in fact, not a matter of definition and theory, but of the historian's practice and art. He must always be aware of the problem. All good historical writing sees the parts in the whole and the whole in the parts.

There have been several attempts at cutting the Gordian knot in a new and indeed striking manner. Suppose we assume that the whole splits up into a number of parts which are essentially self-contained – suddenly the whole problem no longer exists. Let us see history as a series of isolated civilizations. They rise, flourish and decay; thus they succumb to the biological law of all organic life. There is no universal history except the total of a number of unconnected civilizations, a total which is nothing but a mere sum, an adding up. We may, of course, differ about the number, the nature, the limits of these civilizations; but that would be nothing but the ordinary discussion of historical questions between scholars. It seems such an obvious explanation, and Oswald Spengler's stirring book *The Decline of the West* (1918–23) launched the idea in a forceful and ingenious, though at the same time artificial and amateurish, way. But although the idea that a civilization is an independent and self-contained organism is today very popular, the way Spengler created and neglected civilizations of the past in the best dictatorial manner remains entirely unconvincing. And in denying any coherence and continuity between different civilizations this theory made of history a process, or rather a number of processes, of biological necessity, and nothing else. Man and history alike lost all meaning.

Spengler's methods of cool, mathematical prophecy have become burning passion and Christian mysticism in Nicolas Berdyaev's attempt to give the same biological scheme of history a metaphysical meaning. It is beyond my capacity to produce an adequate résumé, still less a criticism, of Berdyaev's theological philosophy. Yet, his bold and paradoxical thesis of understanding the 'failure of history' as its real meaning, and 'religious transfiguration' as its true goal, is at least an attempt at escaping from the barren Spenglerian cycle of barbarism – culture – civilization (the latter two words used in the German rather than the English sense). However, it is only by theology that Berdyaev overcomes a scheme of history that as such he accepts, while I feel that this basic theory, understood as a view of human history and only as such, is mistaken.

It is, of course, possible to compare in their essentials some, or even all, of such civilizations or societies, and this is the main task which Professor A. J. Toynbee sets himself in his imposing work *A Study of History* (1934–61), a work of amazing scholarship and deep insight. Throughout, an immense amount of learned facts and ingenious ideas is spread out, only insufficiently covered by the all-too-modest title. While I can only praise the great value of this storehouse of historical wisdom, I must express my doubts about a few fundamental facts. Toynbee speaks of a 'relative discontinuity between the lives of different societies', but actually denies any continuity between them, vigorously rejecting the normal scheme of universal history. To take the history of what he calls – by what I believe is a much too restricted name – the Western Society as the outcome of a continuous, and in fact the main, stream of history is to him 'violent distortion of historical facts'. I accept his refusal to tolerate the claim that there is only one Civilization (with a capital C). But when he consequently calls the conquest of the earth by Europe a merely political and economic affair, he not only overlooks the actual advance and intrusion of European civilization into the non-European civilizations, he also refuses to see what it means: that the civilizations, for instance of the East, and their history, have been and are being sub-merged during their lifetime into the ever-growing expansion of universal history.

Professor Toynbee accuses the historians of three fundamental misconceptions, 'the egotistic illusion, the catchword of the "Un-changing East", and the misconception of growth as a movement in a straight line'. I do not deny that these changes have some substance, and it may be good to be reminded of the dangers which lie in each of the three issues. However, fundamentally I still believe that the historians are right, and that Toynbee is not. It will be necessary to qualify one-sided statements, but nonetheless the 'egotistic illusion' of Europe is no mere illusion; the East, though greater in some as-pects than anything Europe has achieved, has, as far as I know, much less of a real continuous history than the West; and if history is no straight line, it is still less a number of closed circles. If there are civilizations which completely die, there are others which do not, and they are the more important ones. In spite of all decline and change, essential elements of the Greek, Roman, Jewish, Indian, Chinese, perhaps even the Babylonian and Egyptian, civilizations are still alive, and probably will never die. They bear witness to the fact that no civilization is historically isolated, that they all belong to what I call the current of universal history. I believe it is the highest and indeed ultimate task of the historian to investigate the tension within the very nature of each civilization, its own particular features on the one hand, the part it plays in the great development of man-kind on the other.

However, I must at once set limits to what I have just said, and not only because I know about my own limits but also from a wider point of view. My subject is 'ancient history', and I am aware of the fact that my idea of it is strongly influenced by a tradition which to some people will look old-fashioned or even obsolete. We may have learnt a great deal about the early Eastern empires, but I believe that their history, however interesting in itself and however important an emanation of man's achievement in general, is of major significance only as far as it is connected – directly or indirectly – with European history which adheres to the tradition of its Mediterranean origin, and which alone can teach us the meaning of history. Thus the

Greeks, the Romans and the Jews are of immensely greater importance, for they are the fathers of 'our' history.

There have been attacks on the 'normal' ways of writing history from quite a different quarter. Voices could be heard maintaining that history cannot be fully explained and understood by reason alone. There were romanticists of various colour, believers in some fundamental and clear plan of history which could be approached on an irrational basis only. Myth and mysticism invaded the field of history. Against the cocksureness of certain positivists among historians this was and is, I think, a useful and important reminder. Very few scholars, however, will be prepared to throw overboard their reasoning and their scientific methods of research, and thus surrender to dogmatic axioms which they have simply to accept. History is more than a mere jumble-shop of events; it is not sufficient to find out what happened here and there and now and then, and to put all these bits together, in order to understand what it is all about. We need a pattern, we must see a purpose – but do we then not leave the field of history and enter that of myth?

Perhaps myth is, or at least can be, a reflection, both veiling and unveiling, of the true meaning of man and man's position in the universe. Myth, Schelling's 'primordial history', is in fact the language of religion, and its voice may be heard behind and beyond all merely human talk. This is true of history too, and even the atheist must, in the end, rely on some sort of myth. A nothing-but-human world, whatever its ethical impulses, will easily become a myth of matter and reason. We must not, at any rate, abase myth by trying to let history speak its language. We must be equally careful to keep history's own realm unharmed. There is one truth only, but there are countless ways, all leading towards it. Myth may draw a veil over the last mysteries which our intellect and imagination are too weak to grasp. The real task is to remain conscious of the underlying fundamental truth, in whatever myth it may be hidden, but at the same time to keep clear of the myth in dealing with the matters of human history. We shall see that this does not mean that religion has no place in the historian's mind, but that in fact it can have the highest possible position.

Thus history can be likened to a landscape of plains and valleys and hills in the foreground, which retreat, gradually and to a great depth, into a far and uncertain but dominating background of snow-bound mountains. The shadows of the mountains fall everywhere, but the life and deeds of man remain in the plain and among the valleys and hills.

3. THE HISTORIAN'S ANCESTRY

Many questions can be put with regard to the true nature of the writing of history. Some generations ago, scholars discussed with great heat whether history was a science, and if not how it could be made into one. How many Laws of History have been discovered and again discarded! We need not renew these discussions. It seems that the ways of writing history are almost as various and manifold as the ways of history itself. And it is just this variety of possibilities, with its share of scholarship and science as well as of art and intuition, that provides the fullest possible extension of historical writing. We may prefer one way or another, but no theory ought to restrict this rich splendour to narrow limits.

It may, however, be useful to single out two kinds of history, both of them belonging to the ancient world, but as different as possible. I propose to say a few words about Thucydides and about the historical books of the Old Testament, not discussing any details of their narratives, but the principles on which they rely. The great Athenian and the anonymous Israelites, even though they both had some predecessors from whom they learnt, nevertheless created something new and became the true ancestors of all historical writing in the European tradition.

Thucydides was the first to realize fully the idea of historical truth and he adapted his methods of research and writing to the finding and expounding of this truth. Thus he discovered the critical (or scientific) method which was soon lost again, to be rediscovered only in the last few centuries, from Vico to Ranke. Thucydides had been brought up in Periclean Athens, that is to say, in a period and a society in which for the first time in European history the traditional religion was attacked and gradually overcome by man's discovery of man's reason. The new spirit of rational enlightenment and the example set, for instance, by the medical writers, led Thucydides to a clear and conscious refusal of Herodotus' uncritical mixture of belief and scepticism and to the exclusion of any superhuman interference in human affairs. He learned, more or less alone among his contemporaries and successors, the ways which human reasoning had to follow in order to find out what had actually happened, and at the same time to draw general conclusions from individual facts. While this was the first decisive experience that shaped his mind, the second was the Great War of Greek history which brought about the downfall of Athens from the height of her most shining greatness to the depth of complete defeat and the beginnings of internal disruption. Thucydides, aware of the importance of the war from its very beginning, and justifying his exclusive concern with that war, became the historian of his own age, facing and investigating the great exploits and the terrible horrors of a time out of joint. His deliberate omissions and the relative historical value of the speeches inserted in his narrative do not diminish his achievement as an objective historian nor his determination to reach that objectivity. He sees human valour and human weakness, and we feel behind his restrained words of admiration and disgust the fire that was burning in his heart. Stronger than his passions are the coolness and clarity of his scrutinizing intellect which, with usually sound conclusions, recognizes the decisive forces beneath the surface of events both past and present. No gods, no hostile fate, such as operate in Herodotus' or Sophocles' world, are responsible, but man himself shaped his fortune and his history. The individual's freedom of will, it is true, is often restricted by the inevitable course taken by human society. Nevertheless, we see in Thucydides the most serious attempt at finding the truth and thus the moral power which can elate or condemn. Beyond this, the great recorder rarely gives a judgement of his own, and his intellectual honesty forbids him to speculate on the road which human history may take. He is satisfied if his work will prove useful to those who want exact knowledge of the past, in order to understand the present and the future as following the same general rules of human life. Here, in the famous phrase (I 22) which ends with the proud claim to have written 'a possession for ever', Thucydides discloses the fundamental pragmatism which with him never becomes pedantic and didactic. It is that pragmatism which is naturally connected with even the most impersonal and impartial kind of historical writing, provided that it does not submit to pure scepticism.

There is no similar historical criticism in the historical books of the Old Testament, and if there is pragmatism it certainly is of a different kind. These books differ to some extent in style, intellectual level, and even in their general ideas; but they have enough in common so that for our purposes we can deal with them as a unity. The historians of Israel knew nothing of the methods discovered by Thucydides, but on the other hand they were equally distinct from their own predecessors, the chronicles of the East and the boastful records of its kings. They reveal, all of them, one thing: God in history. The history of the people of Israel is written as a process of continuous revelation of God's will. Perhaps we may say that a somewhat cognate spirit lives in the Behistun inscription of the great Darius, in which he describes himself as 'the servant of Ahuramazda'. But this is merely a record of the king's successful actions, though seen as achieved through the grace and in honour of the god, while the books of the Bible give the full outlines of the history of a whole people, with all its glories and all its failures. This indeed, I believe, is the only national history known to us in which no real attempt is made to idealize its heroes. The true hero of the story is the whole people, and they are seen with uniform objectivity. Throughout we find a deep understanding of human nature, though not of political issues. Without the knowledge of the methods of historical research, the Jewish historians knew that there is only one aim in writing history, to discover the truth. If history is continuously revealing the power and the purpose of God, then the relationship of man (whether as an individual or a community) to God is the only criterion. There has been no inducement to alter the facts of history and to falsify any human achievements, except for the glory of God. The critical historian must admit that this aim has indeed influenced the Jewish historians, and frequently distorted the historical facts, even that sometimes the glory of their God may have been only another expression of national pride. But such an influence cannot conceal the fact that history is seen here as determined by a God who has outgrown his original features of narrow nationalism and primitive savagery to become the God, not of love, but of justice and sanctity. The statement of Froude that 'history is a voice for ever sounding across the centuries the laws of right and wrong' was put to the test for the first time by the men who wrote the historical books of the Old Testament with the passionate belief that God is just.

Modern historians are the heirs of that double ancestry, thus reflecting the general bequest of Greece and Israel to European civilization. Whatever their personal belief or unbelief, whatever their methods of criticism and research, they have to accept the double challenge brought forth by Thucydides and the Bible. Those who evade the one or the other – and many have tried to do so – commit consciously or unconsciously a sin against the Spirit of History. Nobody can be compelled to look at human affairs exactly as Thucydides did, or to believe in God's eternal revelation through history as did the Israelites. But he must answer their challenges.

4. IS HISTORY USEFUL?

Before I try to make my own position clearer I should like to ask myself and my readers one more question concerning the writing and studying of history, the simple question 'What is the good of it?' Does it help us, as individual human beings or as mankind in general? We realize that no creature but man has a history. We naturally ask whether this privilege is a blessing, or at least if it can be turned into a blessing.

I mentioned pragmatism as a natural attitude of the historian. By that I simply mean that everybody interested in history, whether he writes history himself or only studies historical books, has the wish to learn from history. This certainly does not mean the knowledge of mere facts, the dates of the Roman emperors or the numbers of the men who fought at Agincourt. It will not even be sufficient to know the causes and results of historical events. The student of history wants, although sometimes without being fully aware of it, to gain some knowledge of the course of human affairs which will allow him to draw some conclusions with regard to his own present and future.

This, as it were, general pragmatism must be distinguished from a pragmatism more narrowly restricted, the first representative of which was the Hellenistic historian Polybius. He had learned from Thucydides, and when he speaks of the desirability of writing 'pragmatic' history, he actually means 'factual' history, 'straight' history, dealing chiefly with political and military events.[4] This kind of history, he tells us, may provide pleasure, but its main purpose is that of training and educating the mind of the reader, and in particular of the politician and the scholar. Polybius believes in the immediate usefulness of the knowledge of history: it helps in emergencies, it teaches us to understand the actions of men and the causes of events. It is for this interpretation of the purpose of writing and studying that 'pragmatic' history became synonymous with didactic history.

Hardly anybody still believes that history supplies recipes for our own actions. Very few today hope to extract from history strict laws and rules which we have only to understand in order to avoid the mistakes of earlier generations. Indeed we have grown sceptical as to what at all history is able to teach us. As far as historians and history teachers are concerned, I, for once, full-heartedly agree with the view that they are much like other people. Historians on the whole are bad politicians, especially in times of great changes. I am glad to find such an outstanding historian as the late Master of Trinity, Cambridge, of similar opinion when he writes: 'What will now happen to England in peace and war, the historian is no better able to guess than anybody else.'[5] History gives no prescriptions, and the historian is no Harley Street specialist – although a few historians seem to think they are.

The reason why the teaching of history cannot immediately be changed into a currency for practical use lies deeper. Even if we assume that we know enough of an historical event to compare it directly with a present situation, there still remains a flaw. Pure pragmatism is based on the idea that man is essentially the same, no matter when and where he lives. This is largely an illusion. Even though basic psychological reactions as such may be apparently the

---

[4] My remarks on Polybius are largely based on Professor F. W. Walbank's writings. [He has now published a summary of wide significance: 'Polybius' *Sather Lectures* 42 (1972).]

[5] G. M. Trevelyan *English Social History* (1944), 586.

same in different circumstances, even though man remains man in all possible situations – through all changes of habits, of rules, of intellectual awareness – the impact of man's surroundings in one case can differ so much from that in another that the reaction itself may easily belong to a different province of the mind. In a man who believes that life is continuously under the effects of magic forces, even the most elementary reactions, such as the need for food or the desire to make love, are something fundamentally different from the same wishes in a Christian or an agnostic materialist. The differences diminish, of course, when men and events are compared which are closer to each other in time and nature. In many aspects, though never completely, history repeats itself. If this were not so, all the labours of the historians would be completely meaningless. Thus I certainly do not advocate anything like a historical nihilism. But some healthy scepticism with regard to our capacity to learn from history will be quite proper and to the point.

Such scepticism, however, as I said before, it not everything. In fact, if undiluted, it would be justifiable only in an historian who believes with Gibbon that 'history is little more than a register of the crimes, follies and misfortunes of mankind'. Francis Bacon, on the other hand, said 'history makes men wise'. When Lord Acton wrote his devastating attack on Buckle, he summed up with the words: 'He is neither wise himself, nor likely to be the cause of wisdom in others.' He thus assumed that the author of a book on the *History of Civilization in England* should be wise and able to teach wisdom to others. Lord Acton also quotes Bishop Stubbs' sentence: 'History is likely to make men wise, and is sure to make them sad.' Here we have the knowledge of the 'crimes, follies, and misfortunes', but also the conviction that we ought to be able to learn from them in order to become wiser ourselves. I think these quotations culminate in the words of the great Swiss historian Jacob Burckhardt, who tells us that we become by history 'not clever for another time, but wise for ever'. This 'not clever for another time' does away with any kind of narrow pragmatism and, on the other hand, with Carlyle's claim, typical for the nineteenth century, that all knowledge is but a product of history. It is wisdom, not knowledge, that seems to be the result we should hope to obtain from our occupation with history, although it must be added that the amount of wisdom granted to the individual will very largely depend on the capacity and adaptability of the individual concerned. Lord Acton was a Liberal and an optimist; Burckhardt was a conservative and very definitely a pessimist; of Stubbs I do not know enough, but as a bishop and a Tory he is most certainly strongly distinguished from either Acton or Burckhardt; all three of them, however, were outstanding historians. Their common testimony seems very striking, and should go far to convince us.

It will indeed be worthwhile to write, to read, to study history if we learn to become wise, or at least wiser than we have been before. This, I believe, was in Thucydides' mind when he wrote his sentence about the future mission of his work. And true wisdom, wisdom in the sight of God, is clearly the goal of the whole trend of the Old Testament. If we try to define such wisdom as gained from history the first thing we should ascribe to it is reverence; reverence for the eternal forces which rule the undying struggle of men; reverence also for the greatness and endurance of man, for his achievements as well as his tragic failures. History, more than anything else besides religion, serves the purpose of which Dr Johnson spoke: 'Whatever withdraws us from the power of our senses, whatever makes the past, the distant, or the future, predominant over the present, advances us in the dignity of thinking beings.' The knowledge of history enables us to see human beings, nations, periods, civilizations, in their own and specific nature, and at the same time to recognize the affinity of everything human which forms the link between beings and events separated by long distances in time and space. We see in one both the variety and the unity, and we realize the infinite number of possible roads the history of mankind can take at any moment of its course. We may even learn to understand something of the purpose and meaning of all this, but even if we do not reach this point, we should be wise enough to accept the world as it was and is, to accept our human fate, not as a burden but as a task and a necessity full of hope. The least we ought to learn from history is *amor fati*.

5. THE QUESTION OF HUMAN PROGRESS

The nineteenth century made the great discovery of evolution. But it often took, naturally enough, the optimistic view of taking evolution as a guarantee of, or even as identical with, progress. Perhaps no idea ever had such an influence on historical writing as that of human progress which, though in very different forms, can also be detected behind earlier historical methods. It provides by far the simplest and most satisfactory answer to any question about the meaning of history, and even today, when people have become sceptical of this all-too-optimistic interpretation of history, seeing the horrible state to which mankind has led itself, even today we cannot deny that there is some peculiar force in this idea of human progress, however mistaken it may be in itself. It may be worthwhile to clarify our own thoughts, and to try to get rid of the confusion which, as far as I can see, some of the Darwinists as well as some of their opponents have brought about.

Nobody, of course, can maintain that history shows anything like the organic, gradual, and uninterrupted process of natural evolution. Even though, from the point of view of natural science, Sir Julian Huxley may be right in quoting Villiers de l'Isle-Adam's words: '*L'homme . . . seul dans l'univers n'est pas fini*', this does not mean that human history necessarily follows the course of natural evolution. It seems to me very doubtful whether we can call it true human progress when in the course of time the mind of man becomes more complicated and subtle, as it probably does. Still, what recently has been called the 'Ascent of Man', through millions of years of prehistory to the few thousand years of our history, is a predominant fact. We must only beware of equalizing evolution with progress.

Historia facit saltus. Periods of creative power and enlightened reason alternate with passive and chiefly receptive ages. Times in which the eyes of men are set on the present and future are followed by others which look back to the past. If, therefore, progress never marches on in a straight line, does it perhaps advance in spirals or waves, but none the less still remain progress? Or do the crests and troughs of the waves just equal each other, and does history continuously float about on the same level? We must try to find out, not only about the movement but above all about the substance; not only whether and how but also in what respect, if any, progress may have existed.

We naturally ask when we speak of progress: progress in what? To start with, there is certainly no real progress in the nature of the average individual human being. A person may individually rise above his or her own previous level, but the general level remains static. Nobody can maintain that the physical, moral or intellectual qualities of men, even of those outstanding among them, if compared with their opposite numbers, are today on a fundamentally different level from that in, say, A.D. 1688 or 1066 or 400 B.C. Man has changed in many respects, but he has not become better nor, of course, worse. I also believe, taken all in all, that he has neither become happier or less happy. It is the same with history in general, and it makes, I feel, no difference whether we think of progress as a continuous line or as a movement in waves or spirals.

Man is supposed to be a rational being, and to some extent he is. It is, however, simply not true that man has gradually become 'more rational'. Recent events have refuted that view completely. It is, to say the least, doubtful whether reason played a major part in actual historical events and could ever be a proof of progress. Still, later civilizations ought in general to have progressed beyond earlier ones, and later stages of one large period of history beyond earlier stages – but is it real progress? There are between the various periods of history differences in one way or another, but there are no general improvements, for instance, in politics, social order, or artistic, intellectual, spiritual achievements. Who would like to assert that there was progress from Athenian democracy to the absolutism of Louis XIV, from Plato to Hobbes, from the Parthenon to Liverpool Cathedral or even to Westminster Abbey, from the Roman empire under the Antonines to the horrors of the conquest of Peru and Mexico or the disgraces of the Industrial Revolution, from the early Christians to the Inquisition, from Marx and Nietzsche to Hitler? It seems simply ridiculous to claim a general progressive trend in history.

But, many will object, man has immensely increased his power over the forces of nature. No doubt he has. And I am not going to deny any claim of this sort of progress by saying the obvious, and indicating that the realization of so many technical dreams of man has only created the machinery of total war. This is due to a lack of progress, not in technical civilization but in human nature. But is the progress of man's technical skill and power of a fundamental character, that is, a progress of essence and not only of extent? I should like to quote a few sentences.

> There are many great forces in the world, but man's is the greatest. He conquered all space to the boundaries of the Earth, and he made use of the earth in every possible way, being able to dominate all other creatures. He is the only being gifted with language, he alone knows how to protect and enrich his life continuously. He has even succeeded in healing what seemed to be incurable diseases, and there is nothing but death that he cannot conquer.

These lines were written, everybody will guess, some time before man learnt to fly. But not only that, they were actually written in 442 B.C., though I have deliberately altered the poetical language of the choral song from Sophocles' *Antigone* into a sort of colourless prose, without altering the meaning, because I wanted to show that pride in human achievements was essentially the same then as it is now. This pride need not have been belief in progress, and the poet, in the following lines, laments that all the great achievements of man have not led him to the knowledge of good and evil. I fear things have not changed since. No new invention or discovery has ever been made, no new victory won over nature, which did not imply both blessing and misery. It is undoubtedly progress to be able to switch on the electric light instead of striking a spark out of a stone, but primitive man not only never got an electric shock when his implements were rotten, as we sometimes do; his was undoubtedly the greater happiness when he got his fire burning. T. R. Glover once wrote: 'Many things have been done by later men which the men of Periclean Athens could not have done, but a large proportion of these things they might not have thought worth the doing.' Most of them are included in what today is called 'technology'. Though in many ways life may have become easier, there is the obvious danger that we are becoming the slaves of technology, that in fact technology is becoming technocracy, that is to say, rule and tyranny by technical advances, linked with the power of the mass media. This remains true though we might distinguish between the many and the few, for the rise of the masses in the last two centuries has certainly brought about a widespread advancement in various spheres of life.

We should perhaps make an exception for the medical art and accept Sophocles' estimate. Here not only progress, but also the beneficial effects on the life of man, are unquestionable and spectacular. It is true that the path to final deliverance from one kind of suffering frequently led through much individual suffering, and sometimes even brought about new dangers and new diseases. But what even in Hippocrates' time so deeply impressed the poet that he praised it as man's highest achievement has grown through the centuries, even though not without grave setbacks, and has given help and healing to countless sufferers. The ingenuity and heroism of many medical explorers have not been wasted. Even death had to give way and to retreat to a more backward position. There *has* been progress, and yet, may we not ask whether it is *pure* progress? We are living through one of the greatest biological revolutions of the human race: the artificial regulation of the birthrate and the growing extension of human life through medical art, though to be actually old may be anything but a blessing. Anyway, the result will be that mankind on average grows older and older, and if not mankind as a whole, certainly the peoples of the Western world. This means that they are gradually being driven back by 'younger' peoples, and whatever the consequences, a great deal of our European civilization will disappear under the impact of these new conditions. Change there is and will be, but is it progress? We must, at least, put the question, even though we probably shall admit that to our present view, limited as it is, the gains seem to surpass any possible losses.

With even more justification we may attribute the name of progress to another feature of human evolution. It seems a fact that both technically and spiritually the peoples of the earth are drawing nearer to one another. Even the most extensive and most horrible wars cannot refute this fact; on the contrary, they confirm it by being worldwide themselves. But apart from war, there is a tendency to

learn about each other and to come together, a tendency to overcome mountain and sea as well as national barriers, a tendency towards unification of the whole earth. That tendency may still be very
feeble and will suffer serious setbacks, but it is there and it is growing.
This trend towards some sort of unity or solidarity can be revealed
in various aspects of life of which I am not going to speak. I want to
stress only one point which I consider fundamental.

The most conspicuous outward signs of the developments mentioned are the attempts to create some sort of international order in
politics. They may be successful or they may be not. They may mean
progress, because they facilitate peace and order as well as intellectual
and spiritual exchange; or they may mean the opposite because they
destroy national achievements and force national forces into hostile
and dangerous antagonism. We must be very careful before we
decide that any international order means true progress, and is not
only a matter of business interests or, on the other hand, an Utopian
idol. But we should realize that there is very much more in it than
Leagues and Courts and Committees, even more than international
police forces and schemes for feeding mankind materially or spiritually. Behind all this there is a fact of the first magnitude, the fact
that there exists a common social and international conscience, and
that its power has been increasing, however slowly, for a very long
time. It too has suffered, and indeed is suffering, very grave setbacks; but it always survived and grew. We are used to speaking of
Christian standards; indeed, the influence of Jesus' teaching and of
the unity of Medieval Christendom were essential in the shaping
of these standards. But they are, in fact, both more and less than
Christian, more because they belong, or at least tend to belong, to all
mankind, less because they are distinct from religion.

I identify these standards with common conscience; for even the
best moral standards and highest ideals, such as that of the brotherhood of mankind, are dead words unless they are fully alive in the
conscience of men, both individuals and communities. No conscience
is absolute and abstract, and the conscience of nations is very far from
it. Up to now history has been, to a very large extent, national
history, and no historian in his senses will be so blind or ideological
as to deny any nation the right of being proud of the greatness of its

history. It seems to me a weakish and quietist feeling that coined the phrase 'Happy the country which has no history'. History makes a nation, and nations make history. It is unlikely or, to say the least, very far off, that history will ever remove the nations as essential sections of mankind. But a nation is more than the nationalism of its members, and the greatest nations of all times were and are those which outgrew their own nationalism and, in serving their own purposes, created something that belongs to mankind.

This leads us to the story of common conscience. Just as in earlier times the individual human being had duties towards the community in which he lived, whether village, tribe, class or city, duties which he learnt gradually to take not as a compulsion but as a responsibility, so the individual and, in fact, the community too came under the growing sway of wider responsibilities, of obligations due to those outside their immediate local or social or political neighbourhood. How many barriers and frontiers have fallen during the centuries of the past, how many gaps been filled and gulfs bridged, in order that men of different origin, different class, different outlook, might come to know, to appreciate, and sometimes even to love, one another. The neighbour whom we were told to love, gradually grew, first into our fellow-countryman and finally into the distant figure of our human brother in general. It is a fact that the social conscience of mankind has grown and is growing, both in intensity and extension. There is no need for examples to prove this; in spite of many serious setbacks it is obvious that inside each nation one barrier after another is falling. Men, of course, do not become equal; there will always be those who rule, and those being ruled, and cultural leadership must remain with the minority. But the solidarity and unity of the whole nation in each country has increasingly become very much more than a patriotic slogan; it is becoming reality, because it has become the task of the conscience both of each individual and the community as a whole. Here – that at least is our hope, however distant the final goal – is one of the strongest forces that will shape the future.

Parallel to this gradual awakening and growing of social conscience grows, as a younger and weaker plant, international conscience. 'It is,' Charles Morgan says, 'open to us to claim, if we will, that in a thousand years political understanding, if not yet political application, of the idea of common humanity has made some advance.' Here too, mankind is on its way to unity, or rather solidarity, although our own experience with its fierce revival of nationalism may indicate the opposite; at any rate, the final goal is still very far ahead. This dual process, as it were, accompanies the course of history, and it may well be that something of the meaning of history is revealed through it. Here we are allowed to speak of real progress, and we shall not destroy the joyful hope of this thought by the fear that this progress, too, will involve disadvantage and loss. We found before that even though we cannot believe in pure and full progress in other aspects, the gain may sometimes outweigh the loss. I am convinced that this is even more true in this last issue. Whatever the dangers of social democracy (and they are more than a few), however strong and justified our fear of a society planned and governed by a bureaucracy, however strongly we believe that every century is, above all, the century of its great men – in a way the 'Century of the Common Man' is the necessary outcome of previous centuries in which so many political and social restrictions and deprivations had to go. On the other hand, civilization, literature, art, even to an extent scholarship and philosophy, have been, and probably always will be, both national and élitist. But whatever such national achievements may lose by their incorporation into an international and democratic order, or rather by their acknowledging the standards of an all-human conscience, they will win more. This, in the end, cannot be proved until it happens. But if we believe in it, we shall be able to overcome scepticism and pessimism, and find the way to a truer understanding of the meaning of history.

6. THE QUESTION OF TRADITION

Most of what is commonly called progress is nothing but change. All historical changes, whether small or large in scope and effect, are partial changes. Even the greatest revolutions – and by the expression 'revolution' we indicate a sudden and fundamental change – do not do away with everything that was before, and they usually end in a reversal which revives much of what had been before. There is always a clash between the forces of change and those of continuity, and we may indeed say that all history is a continuous struggle between these two kinds of forces. During some periods things seem almost completely under the sway of vehement changes, while in others the power of continuity overrules everything else, and again in others the forces from both sides are keeping a fair balance. There is no period which is not shaped to some extent by either force. The struggle is always going on, just as Zoroaster's struggle between good and evil, silently and secretly or openly and noisily. It seems correct to say that this struggle is the very substance of all historical movement. But for this very reason, just because it goes on in an unending up and down, it is obviously quite senseless – unless we detect a definite trend in the eternal movement. This would, in fact, reveal the meaning behind the meaningless, the meaning of history.

We saw that progress can be claimed, if at all, to a small extent only as the exponent of this meaning, although it certainly results from a combination of the forces of continuity and those of change. Progress, according to its essential nature, looks ahead; therefore change is stronger in it than continuity. But even when by some sort of miracle or through an ingenious piece of mental endeavour, the mixture of forces appears to be harmonious, even when it reaches the perfection of Hegelian dialectics, the question whether the outcome is true progress or only an advance in one direction which is coupled with a retreat in another, usually remains unanswered.

Let us try to look at the other side of the picture. What happens if the clash of the forces leads to a clear predominance for the conservative side? The outcome then is tradition, which, just as much as progress, derives from a mixture of continuity and change, in this case with continuity as the stronger partner. Tradition looks back, though not only back, just as progress looks ahead, though not only ahead. Historians have been called 'prophets with their faces turned backwards'. This seems only another way of saying that tradition is the essence of history and must have something to do with its deeper meaning. We ask whether this is true.

There is one kind of tradition with which the historian is particularly concerned. That is the tradition of historical evidence, the handing down of the knowledge of events, remembered, retold, rewritten, from one generation to another. This handing down is the very substance of tradition, as expressed in the original meaning of the Latin *tradere*. Tradition in this sense, however, is nothing but the handmaiden of history, *ancilla historiae*. It provides the supply by which historical scholarship and the historical imagination are fed. But this kind of tradition, indispensable as it is for every sort of historical writing, has no value or meaning of its own. A Greek papyrus or a Roman inscription, a medieval chronicle or a recent diplomatic report – they all have their small place in history, they will all have their particular beauty or significance as well as their particular shortcomings, but as parts of tradition they are devoid of sense unless they are studied and interpreted by a historian. Such tradition provides the most valuable tools of historical scholarship, but it is no living part of the tradition which is supposed to be at the core of history.

Tradition as the great *basso continuo* which accompanies history is a very complex thing. We are used to speaking of living and dead traditions, we know tradition as something magnificent, striking, glorious, and we know of traditions which are trivial or downright silly. But even a dead tradition must have been alive before, and many of the petty customs which hide behind the idea of tradition were once revered and perhaps sacred. Views on traditions vary equally. To one man a certain act may be a holy rite or an eloquent symbol which to another man appears as an obsolete relic of the past. Pious faith declares: 'Remember the days of the old, consider the years of many generations. Ask thy father, and he will show thee; thy elders, and they will tell thee' (*Deut.* 32:7). Naïve and thoughtless traditionalists speak of the good old days. But Goethe thunders: 'Woe's thee, that thou'rt the heir of Time.'[6] Dickens denounces the horrible traditions of social injustice and negligence, and Shelley the stale traditions of bourgeois life.

We try to find our way out of this embarrassing and irritating hubbub of contradictory voices. When we dealt with the idea of progress we found that progress hardly ever fully exists in history.

[6] This is Mr A. G. Latham's translation of 'Weh dir, dass du ein Enkel bist' (*Faust* I).

Remarks on the meaning of history

Progress is to a large extent an illusion, tradition is not. There can be no doubt about it: whether for good or ill, it does exist.

Tradition is the memory of the human race. According to a charming story by Anatole France, a story not historical and yet true in a deeper sense, Pontius Pilate, when asked by a friend years after Jesus' death, could only answer: '*Je ne m'en souviens plus.*' The individual forgets even important facts, tradition remembers. The individual dies, tradition lives on. But it lives on only because human beings preserve it. The explanation for this paradox is that tradition is entirely and exclusively a matter of human communities. Community life creates tradition, and the continuance of this life during many generations preserves it. Family and state, village and tribe, school and church, guild and regiment – they and other communities are the homes in which traditions live.

In certain human activities tradition is of particular strength. The conservative force contained in all kinds of religious worship is well known, and countless facts in the history of Greek and Roman religion seem to confirm this at least as strongly as the evidence of the Christian church. In many ways the ancient peoples displayed a deeper influence of, and a stricter adherence to, tradition than later ages. While tradition in the fine arts (which involved a craft) is a common feature at almost all times – it is significant that we habitually speak of schools of painting and sculpture – it is not the same with poetry. Still, Greek and Roman poetry were to a very large extent products of tradition. Greater and lesser poets alike, in every particular kind of poetry, were tied to certain rules and ideas, frequently very important rules and fundamental ideas. Perhaps the most amazing example is the use of the Doric dialect, which was traditional for choral odes, within the framework of Attic tragedy. It is almost as if certain poetical parts in Shakespeare's plays were regularly written in French, though it is obvious that Greek tragedy was also a religious act and bound to certain religious traditions. This example makes it abundantly clear what an outstanding part tradition can play in the building-up of a work of art. But it shows equally that the greatness of the final work depends on very much more than mere tradition. It seems hardly necessary to expound that statement which is almost self-evident.

I believe we are justified in drawing from this example a more general conclusion. Tradition and revolution are the two great phenomena which shape the whole course of history, or rather keep history going, though neither of them nor their combined effort, whether they fight each other or act simultaneously, are capable of filling history with any specific contents or giving it a general meaning. If we think of the last two great revolutions, the French and the Russian, their different natures and different results are obvious; but equally obvious are the effects of different traditions from which they arose. Again and again we find tradition broken and upset by revolution, and revolution checked and overcome by tradition – proof enough that neither of them is strong enough alone to determine the whole course of history. Their eternal alternation, on the other hand, the Heraclitean rhythm of opposites coming forward in turn, is apt to be misunderstood as a proof to the contrary, as a symbol of the complete senselessness of history.

Historians may be traditionalists or they may be not. The fact that grants tradition its grandeur and, even when it is irrelevant, its justification, lies in its one outstanding quality: it is witness of history. It reminds us that history is alive and has something to tell us. But no tradition can tell us what this something is. Tradition is a witness but not a judge or a jury. No verdict is uttered, no truth revealed. We are back to where we were before.

7. GOD IN HISTORY

In approaching the final part of our investigation we are advancing onto difficult ground. For we shall come across so many beliefs and half-beliefs, and we shall probably have to rely on one or two of them ourselves, that our reasoning may find itself lost. However, I hope I shall find my way through that limited stretch of a very large country which alone I propose to explore.

I mentioned the two methods of writing history as represented by Thucydides and the Old Testament. Their outcomes with regard to the meaning of history can be summed up as a reasoned scepticism or general pragmatism on the one hand, a belief in God as revealed in and through history on the other. It is natural as well as a decisive question whether any union between these two interpretations of history is possible, and – since the possibility has proved its existence in the minds and the works of many a historian – whether we can express in clear words the product of that union, which would be nothing short of an interpretation of the meaning of history.

Without being so immodest as to apply the concluding clause of the following quotation to my own limited reasoning, I believe it is appropriate here. It comes from a book by the late Professor C. E. Raven.[7] 'It was not until the Biblical and the Hellenistic valuation of nature as God's realm and of history as God's acts came again to be accepted, when the scientific movement set itself to see life steadily and see it whole, that any integral and integrative philosophy could be recovered.' Even if we should agree with the words of Professor (now Sir) G. N. Clark, which sound almost like a rebuttal of the earlier quotation, that the work of historical research 'is not to see life steadily and see it whole, but to see one particular portion of life right side up and in true perspective',[8] even then every historian as a historian, and not only as a human being in general, must see something behind and beyond that particular portion of life. Otherwise he will hardly be able to see things 'in true perspective'. If we therefore apply Raven's sentence and the quotation from Matthew Arnold's lines on Sophocles[9] – as far as that is possible – to our specific subject, this would mean that history will not be seen as the whole it is, unless we comprehend to the full the union of Greek and Biblical thought which I mentioned before. For us at this point of our investigations, for us especially as disciples of the critical methods of the last four or five generations of historians, and lastly of Thucydides, this can mean only one thing, and that is to find out what is God's part in history.

To a non-scientist like myself it seems very much easier to recognize God's work in nature than in history. Perhaps the belief that God is revealed in every part of the natural world, in the plan of the universe as well as in the millions of differently shaped stars in a snowflake, often leads to a pantheism which practically puts Nature into

[7] *Good News from God* (1943), 56.
[8] *Historical Scholarship and Historical Thought* (1944), 11.
[9] *Sonnet to a Friend*: '. . . who saw life steadily and saw it whole.'

God's place. But even then the belief in a divine power, living and working in nature, is at the bottom of it. The pantheist fights on the side of God. Fortunately it is not my task to discuss the philosophical or religious attitude of modern scientists. My only – and simple – question is whether God, if there is a God, is revealed in history. There seems little doubt that the history of man's unending tragedies, follies and failures, even though they may alternate with achievements and greatness, is in no sense divine – indeed how could it be? Man may be God's creation; history is man's, the creation of the creature. Therefore we simply cannot expect that we should be able to recognize God in the men who make history, or in the events which are its substance. If God acts in history at all, he will follow a purpose of which we know nothing. We may try to guess something, though our guesses will be purely subjective views and beliefs. We cannot expect to see God's hand in history in a direct manner, not even in victories of Good over Evil.

I therefore hesitate to identify God with any particular cause in history, and I am doubtful of attempts to see God's action in the particular course of a historical phenomenon. Even though there may be a good deal of truth in the old saying that 'the gods blind whom they want to destroy', it is hazardous to accept this as a rule for the interpretation of historical facts. Thus I cannot accept the argument which runs on the following lines:[10] Napoleon in 1812 wanted to defeat the Russian power by an advance into the heart of the country; the Russian generals tried to stop his advance by opposing him in open battles, although they were always defeated. Both acted therefore contrary to their own interests, but unwittingly brought about the final outcome. This shows, it is argued, that what really happens in history is of God's, and not man's, making. I am afraid there are many examples to prove the exact opposite. The event seems too small and at the same time viewed from too moralistic a standpoint. For though it may have seemed necessary to beat and eliminate the tyrannical emperor, it seems more than doubtful whether the Russian Tsar was more in accordance with the future course of history (or, as to that, with God's purpose) than the heir of the French Revolution. There is, on the other hand, some truth in the idea that we must look

[10] P. Leon *Hibbert Journal* 42 (1943/4), 254 ff.

for the paradoxical facts in history in order to see behind them. Polybius, a great historian though not a genius like Thucydides, realized that the paradox (τὸ παράδοξον τῶν πράξεων) is the only exciting thing in history, and he therefore made it his *Leitmotif*. He saw Tyche working behind the scene, and this deity – Fate and Chance in one – is the agnostic's word for God, though for a God devoid of purpose, a deity that could be malignant as well as benevolent. One might think with Thomas Hardy that 'the President of the Immortals (an Aeschylean phrase) ended his sport with Tess'. Still, there may have been some very great 'miracles' in history which it is hard to understand and to explain. I put inverted commas round that word deliberately. Even in the case of such 'miracles' we must be very careful. We can never be certain where in history the demarcation line (if there is one, as I believe there is) really runs between God's will and the playful irrationalism of chance. The only standard we have, apart from the inexplicable character of a historical phenomenon, whether man or event, is the possible meaning behind the facts. I need hardly say how difficult it can be to find that out. We must try to avoid moralistic attitudes which may or may not be fitting to certain human standards, but may be entirely outside God's possible concern. We must try to find out whether there is some necessary impact upon the general trend of history, in particular towards the distant, but I trust growing, solidarity of mankind which, if anything, ought to be in some way the ultimate trend of human history.

It will be understood, I dare say, that what I call a miracle in history is nothing outside the laws of nature. It is the paradoxical character of the facts, combined with their intrinsic importance, that creates a historical miracle. Can we, for instance, apply this expression to the victory of the small Greek states over the large Persian empire? Perhaps. That victory certainly made history. It saved Europe, and everything Europe was to stand for in the days to come. We should hardly have become Europeans in the sense which we attribute to the word if the people from a few Greek city-states had not fought and conquered at Marathon and Salamis and Plataea. It seems more difficult to decide whether Rome's survival after Cannae had a similar significance, though possibly it had. For Carthage, although strongly under the influence of Hellenistic civilization, was not capable of building up that unity of the Mediterranean world which seems to have been the distant goal of history since the days when Phoenicians and Greeks settled on its shores in East and West, that unity eventually achieved in the *Pax Augusta* of the Roman empire. There are, of course, many other examples of such decisive historical events, some of a purely negative character, as, for instance, the burning of the library of Alexandria, which lowered the cultural level for centuries to come.

To mention a somewhat similar 'miracle' of later times, I should like to think of the amazing coincidence in the age of the Renaissance and the Reformation of the discoveries or rediscoveries of new continents, of the literature and civilization of Classical antiquity, and of the Gospels. Only through their combined impact came about that modern world of ours to which the Roman Catholic church, the ruler of the medieval world, also succumbed.

Another kind of historical miracle is the appearance of a great man whose life work could remain unfinished and even could be an obvious failure, but who has nevertheless anticipated the essential features of a new epoch of history. Thus Alexander's empire was soon destroyed, and his idea of uniting, one way or another, East and West was abandoned in favour of the foundation of several independent states and the expansion of Greek civilization, spread in a way beyond and even against Alexander's own ideas. Later, however, action was followed by reaction, and the East soon sent its indestructible religious forces to meet Greek rationalism and secularism, and to strengthen the irrational forces left within the Greek mind. East and West joined, or did not join but at least lived together, in the syncretistic Hellenistic world which then found a new ruler to unite it into one empire. Rome became Alexander's successor.

It was in a sense similar with Caesar. He was murdered because he aimed at a form of empire and monarchy which the Republic – dying as it was, but not yet dead – could not accept. It was his absolutism, unRoman in appearance and essence, that united against him such different minds as were to be found among the conspirators. Augustus, with his clever design of mixing monarchic power and republican appearances, succeeded where Caesar had failed. The greater man was too great for his times. Caesar had tried to anticipate a development which after several intermediate stages eventually found its fulfilment three centuries later, in the rule of Diocletian, the *Dominus et Deus*. Caesar no less than Alexander failed in his own plans and ideas. But both were necessary to lead the way mankind had to go. They hurried forward with a speed which was appropriate to the capacity of a single genius, but not to that of the majority of men. History seems to have been shaped in a distinct and decisive way by both the work and the failure of these two great men. The success of the smaller men who followed them was just as necessary, but it was not they who made the revolutionary changes. However, whether we look at the few very great or the several less great – does it not seem as if they were not the players but the chessmen?

A very different kind of historical paradox is even more striking. Occasionally an idea, a people, a civilization, outlives all human expectation, and continues to maintain its historical existence in spite of the strongest endeavours to destroy it. It is perhaps here that the greatest heroism of human beings is displayed; it is certainly here that we realize more than in anything else the tremendous power of the spirit. The spiritual history of mankind knows of many martyrs who died for the truth in which they believed. Against all oppression by rulers or churches, councils or violent mobs, truth prevailed. Spiritual forces were stronger than political and social powers, but the spirit survived frequently because it was preserved and carried on not only by individuals but by communities of men. Such communities are more than the flesh and blood, more even than the minds and souls, of their members. When peoples and civilizations survive it is again the spirit which plays the decisive part.

Let us look at one or two outstanding examples. I do not know enough about China, the only one among the peoples and civilizations of today which derives from antiquity and is still living as a large community in its old land. Whether the immensity of the country and the multitude of the people were a factor more in favour or in disfavour of China's survival I cannot say. But the perils through which this venerable isolated civilization had to go were of the first magnitude and have not yet ended. If we ask why this happened I can only say that I am convinced China was not preserved for centuries and centuries to become a victim or a mere dependency of Western civilization. Her old wisdom, however adapted to the issues of modern life, may still one day be an essential force in a new shaping of man's spiritual heritage.

Apart from China, there are, as far as I know, only small peoples or in fact mere splinters of peoples, such as the Parsees in India or the gipsies, that have survived from ancient times. To what extent the Greeks of today, with the discord of their politics and the lovable nature of their peasantry, are the descendants and heirs of the ancient Greeks is a highly disputed question, both inside and outside Greece. Philhellenism and patriotism have done their best to revive the picture, usually highly idealized, of ancient Greece, but revival is not survival. At any rate, the history of the Greeks was for many centuries disrupted to such an extent that hardly any feature of ancient Greece is still alive and it is simply impossible to speak of survival. One people, however (if it is a people), one civilization (if it is one) has survived in the midst of the Western world, and its history is beyond any doubt one of the greatest miracles of history. The Jews have existed through most of the history of mankind. 'Stretching from the earliest day to the last, the history of the Jews encloses in its extension that of all our histories.' With a certain qualification, due to our improved knowledge of early times, this sentence of Pascal's still stands.

The subject of the history of the Jews is, I believe, relevant in the highest degree to our general question, and it concerns the Gentiles no less than the Jews. 'The whole content of Judaism', Leo Baeck tells us, 'lies in its unfinished and infinite history', a history based on belief in one God and the rule of moral law. That means that belief in God is combined with belief in man which culminates in belief in mankind. The following short sketch of the history of the Jews owes much to the essay which the great Russo-Jewish historian S. M. Dubnow wrote, about a century ago, under the title *The Jewish History*. His book was called a *Leitfaden*, a manual; my late wife used it to speak of the *Leidfaden*,[11] a sad pun, like most puns not translatable but containing real truth. There is a peculiar and tragic rhythm

[11] Eva Ehrenberg *Sehnsucht – mein geliebtes Kind* (1963), 47 ff.

in Jewish history. With the exile in Egypt began the long line of enslavements and persecutions, and also the equally long history of the relations between the Jews and their 'hosts'. Moses, who bore an Egyptian name, may have been the first great offspring of this spiritual marriage. Ruth, an Arab woman from Moab, became the ancestress of King David. Centuries later the Jews went through the short Babylonian exile. Monotheism was again and finally established, and once again, a great voice was heard among them, Deutero-Isaiah. The restoration under Persian rule created the 'People of the Book', which meant that they were also the People of the Law. They were spiritually strong enough to meet the strongest, in fact the only true opponent of and complement to their own message, Hellas. At that time, the Jews had begun to live outside Palestine which had become too small for them. They settled abroad, in Persia, even in Egypt, and this dispersion culminated in the final Diaspora after the destruction of the temple in A.D. 70. Now no Jewish state survived, as it had existed intermittently during the preceding centuries, no religious centre existed except in the pious minds of the people; but the people themselves did survive, and their book went with them, with the covenant of Mount Sinai, with its code of social ethics, with the passionate preaching of the prophets and the proclamation of ethical monotheism, with the poetry of the psalms, and with the history books which claimed for past and future the unique part played by the people as God's instrument. As early as the third century B.C. the Greek version of the Book, the *Septuagint*, which was to become the Old Testament of Christianity, and later the peculiar Platonism of Philo with its allegorical interpretation of the Bible, witnessed to the endeavours to bridge the gulf between Israel and Hellas.

The later history of the Jews, though outside the limits of ancient history (and of which I know little at first hand), shows even more clearly the alternation of isolation and persecution of the Jews, and the happy coexistence with other peoples. This alternation brought with it temporary waverings in the Jewish mind between a growing orthodoxy and an open attitude towards general civilization. First in the Arabian East, then for centuries in Spain and Portugal, the Jews flourished under régimes which maintained tolerance and high cultural standards. Great names like those of Maimonides and Spinoza indicate the spiritual nature of the mutual give and take, which can be truly described as a marriage between reason and faith. Surprisingly, the Jewish contribution now was chiefly one of reasoning and dialectic knowledge rather than religious beliefs; in the West the Jews had, in a sense, taken over the part of the Greeks, while in Eastern Europe they accepted and transformed the mysticism of their neighbours. In medieval England, France and Germany the Jews never found that freedom which would have given them a real share in the life of these countries. And sooner or later they were forced through persecution to take up their wanderings again. For the Jews the Middle Ages, with their social isolation and lack of political rights, ended – or should we rather say, seemed to have ended – as late as 1789. The great century of European, especially German, Jewry followed, only to lead to the most extensive and most barbarian persecution of all times. But, in the words of Dean Inge, 'the Jews have stood beside the graves of all their persecutors'. They have proved what has been called the paradox of survival through persecution.

The dispersion and the wanderings of the Jews are unique in history. Their communities throughout the world were never independent colonial cities such as those of the Greek diaspora, nor were the Jews citizens of a ruling state like the Romans and the British in their diaspora. For the Jews the diaspora was a source of unending suffering, and if they survived, thanks both to their tribal coherence and to stubborn loyalty to their faith, they paid their tribute not only in blood and tears, but also in a distortion of character. Most laws of the community became rigid and petty, essentially a ritual, even though they never lost the coherence with their great tradition. Through their history, and in particular through the restrictions imposed by the Gentiles – church, state and society – the nature of the Jews, and of the Jewish community as a whole, changed. A people which for many centuries had been, apart from a class of priests and 'intellectuals', a people of farmers and soldiers, craftsmen and traders, were forced into becoming money-lenders and usurers, and thus acquired the reputation of sinister and greedy Shylocks within a world of easy-going Antonios and Bassanios.

The same history of the Jews throughout the ages is also full of wise thinkers, clever scholars, saintly martyrs and simple believers. They maintained the purity and the spiritual discipline of their faith. They, poor vagrants, passed through the histories of other peoples, and one of these meetings was without important effects on either side. Some of the Jews succumbed to the great and natural temptation to break down the barriers and submerge in the world of the other peoples, to become 'assimilated'. This is part of the temporary union which occurred wherever the Jews were allowed to take root. No human intention and no meaningless fate could ever have contrived such a gigantic scheme.

Other Jews succumbed to the equally great temptation of following the nationalistic trend of the other peoples. Natural pride in the achievements and the history of the Jews combined with an urgency to help the poor and persecuted masses, first of Eastern and then of Central Europe, to promote Zionism. We owe reverence to the undying nostalgia for the old country which as a mystical force accompanied the Jews through centuries of their post-Biblical history. We pay homage to the great and amazing work which Zionism has performed, and is performing, in the new home in Israel. I am convinced that it is necessary to make life possible both for those who will go there and for those who will not. But in spite of all this, I cannot share the belief that it is an essential task of the Jews to make Israel a state like other states, and to add one more nationalism to all the others which do their utmost to destroy mankind.

The Jews are still the chosen people, not of course because they are better (or worse) than others, not even because they were the first to proclaim spiritual monotheism, although this is a fact of primary importance, and not only because they believed in the unity of mankind and the coming of the Messiah. It is their fate which makes them really unique, and this fate, as reflected in their survival and history, is to be a community without a lasting home, destined to teach mankind through their very existence the eternal truth of the existence of God. It was, after all, not 'odd of God to choose the Jews'!

Jewish stubbornness and unbelief have had to be overcome time and again, ever since the days of Moses. The suffering of the Jews may be due to their own as well as other people's misdeeds, though there can be no doubt that the greater guilt lies with their enemies. In truth, it is not a question of guilt, for we must realize that it is part of God's plan concerning man. It is a lasting signpost on the road which slowly but steadily may lead towards the unification of mankind. This is also the reason why I hesitated, though probably mistakenly, to call the Jews, dispersed as they are by Providence, a people, and Judaism a civilization. Jewish history is essentially different from all other histories, because it is not also the history of a land, and because, apart from outside interference, it is not divided into epochs. 'The Jew,' says Franz Rosenzweig, 'by having his own eternity, makes time a powerless servant of eternity.' If the unique part played by the Jews in human history can hardly be understood unless we see in it the outcome of a divine purpose, this must be particularly true of the moment when from the Jewish community originated what can be called the greatest revolution of European history.

Intentionally I did not speak at an earlier stage of Jesus and the origins of Christianity. It is with the greatest hesitation, as a non-Christian, and in a very restricted aspect only, that I am now going to do so, and I do not wish to repeat what I have said previously in this book. The essence of Christendom, if I am not mistaken, is that God became Man, and thus the greatest of miracles, completely incomprehensible by reason alone, became part of human history. Since the days when Jesus' disciples believed in Jesus as the Messiah, in the Incarnation and the Resurrection, millions have shared this belief, and have lived and died for it and in it. This belief has become a historical fact of the first magnitude, but it is based on a story which is beyond the categories of history. If the belief of the millions is true, if we have to accept the fact that the Son of God lived and died as a human being, then we have to realize that here history is inseparably interwoven with the eternal, that for once, but only for once, the paradox became real: the absolute was historical and history was absolute. In my view, only those who share the belief in this paradox have the right to argue about it. Others must, and indeed have the right to, leave the interpretation of this miracle to those who cannot but see history in the light of this one overwhelming fact. For them, the earthly life of the Lord and the Resurrection have become the only and true centre of human history. Previous ages have to be recognized in their growth towards this centre, later seen as radiating from it, to lead to the final end which Christ has foretold. The meaning of history is thus settled once and for all, although our imperfect and erring human judgement may disagree about many of its particular details.

However, even if the birth of Christianity is understood merely as one of the events of human history, even if understood as such and not as the wholly miraculous incarnation of the eternal within the historical, it remains one of the greatest events. Even in the sense in which I have used the word 'miracle' before, this is indeed the greatest among them. We have learnt to understand better than previous generations its historical presuppositions and parallels, because we have learned more about its times, about the unity of the Hellenistic oecumene and the Roman empire, and the variety of social, intellectual and spiritual standards and aims, about the whole fascinating picture of an epoch in which the most heterogeneous forces were involved. However, all this, though it helps one to understand many details, does not explain what has been called the tremendous success of Christianity, which to many seemed and still seems the greatest miracle. There can be little doubt that it was mainly due to the unique personality of Jesus. 'There has never been any like Him before or since, never, up to a miracle. For that is the miracle that there never was nor ever will be another like Him.' This is the voice of belief; it is Dostoevsky's voice. Apart from the certainty about the future, which is beyond the competence of historical scholarship, there is, however, the fact, confirmed again and again by modern theologians and historians, that the Jesus of the Gospels and St Paul is not the true historical Jesus. Was he the Essene of the Dead Sea Scrolls or the rebel against Rome, the long-expected Messiah or simply a social reformer? We do not know. But the historian can and must agree with Dostoevsky, if we speak of the effects of his personality, which were enormous.

But Christianity, as soon as it was Christianity and no longer a Jewish religious sect, was no longer simply the teaching of Jesus. From the day when St Paul preached to the Gentiles, and the Evangelists had written the Gospels, the claim grew that the

Kingdom of God was to fill the earth and overcome the kingdom of man. But the growing church was no *Civitas Dei*, and when Constantine united state and church it lost any claim to be of the other world. Christianity suffered the fate of every great spiritual movement in that it grew and spread, was organized and deteriorated. The history of the Christian church is almost as foolish and blood-stained as the history of the state.

This could also be said of Islam, which in an even shorter time than Christianity in Europe overwhelmed churches and non-churches in the Middle East which the Arabs overran with their warriors and their religion. Mohammed, their great prophet, was believed to be the heir to Abraham and Jesus. The advent of Islam was a revolution as great as the Christian. At the same time Buddhism started to fill the Far East. What Buddha had taught was the opposite of Judaism as well as of its 'children', Christianity and Islam. Instead of the commandments and the preaching of love towards one's neighbours, Buddhism was the faith in personal redemption only, ultimately a matter of spiritual egotism rather than of altruistic brotherhood. Four different religions had arisen, not bound to any ethnic frontiers. Together they brought happiness and misery to the majority of mankind.

We return to Europe and the Christian church. What we have said before is of course not the whole story, and no verdict would be more mistaken than to condemn the church on its record of crime and sin. The miracle of Christianity would be a very poor affair if the widespread and almost complete victory of the new religion over the pagan world was nothing but an outward change. The church, in all its troubles and vicissitudes, stood for those values which lived on in the immortal language of the Prophets, the Psalter and the Gospels, just as Islam lives on in its Koran. Christianity also stood for those values which were proclaimed and discussed in the works of Plato, Aristotle, and the Stoa. Above all, the voice of Jesus was never silenced, and time and again it rose triumphantly over the clamour of dispute and the distortion by friends and foes alike. Time and again it preached among the peoples and nations the unity and brotherhood of mankind.

It is probably true that the decline of Christianity during the cen-

turies since the Renaissance and in particular during the nineteenth
and twentieth centuries – a decline by no means without interrup-
tions and creative recoveries, but a decline nevertheless – has something to do with the lowering of human standards which led to the
horrors of Nazism and also to that 'inertia of the heart' (*Trägheit des
Herzens*) which is responsible for so much of the misery of our age.
There are many today who think that the situation demands a front
against both materialism and humanism. I object to this combination, although I am aware of the fact that humanism shared some of
the faults and shortcomings of materialism. I believe that humanism
is neither dead nor ripe to die, but, based not only on literary and
aesthetic values but also on natural science, has to find a new way to
restore the dignity of man. This way will lead through the humility
which realizes man's failures rather than through the pride in his
achievements. Humanism of whatever shape and shade will be an
important part of the contribution of the Western world to the
future, and if there is to be a revival of religion – of which so much is
said these days – there must also be a revival of humanism.

Christianity, or 'Christian standards' as it is usually called, have
been primarily concerned with the rights and duties of the individual
within the community, whether the thought centred round the
'immortal soul of every human being' or the 'Rights of Man'. We
have learnt anew to attribute the highest possible value to these
ideas, since we have realized how they have been trampled underfoot
in a country that deliberately waged war against the traditions of
Christianity and humanism. It was possible for one of the great
nations of Europe, in a state of mental disease, to renounce those
traditions. This clearly shows that they were not strong enough. It is
true that the rights of one individual involve obligations for the
other. But to what extent the demand for selflessness, self-sacrifice –
in short: love – has remained unfulfilled is shown by the outstanding
features of what is left of European civilization today: the worship
of power (both in nationalism and totalitarianism), the worship of
matter and material, the worship of money and prosperity (both in
capitalism and communism), the worship of mere numbers (in and
outside politics), the worship of the body (sport, sex, eugenics), the
worship of science, engineering, machinery, efficiency. I do not wish

to be misunderstood. I call these various topics features, not evils, of our civilization. The point I wish to make is that all these things have become 'worship'. We use our capacity of reverence in wrong directions, and we are about to lose that 'awe' which Athena in Aeschylus' *Eumenides* warns the citizens never to expel from the state. Goethe says: '*Das Schaudern ist der Menschheit bester Teil.*'[12] As long as the obligations of man remain what they are in our society and our way of life, the mere counterpart of his rights, as long as our laws are largely based on respect for the rights of man and not more decisively on the acknowledgement of his duties towards society, it is difficult to imagine that our civilization can still be saved from committing suicide.

I have gone further than I originally intended to go, and I shall probably be blamed for not sticking to my last. However, if I am not mistaken, these reflections have led to a coincidence, quite unexpected so far as my own intentions were concerned. The evidence for God's purpose in history coincides with the knowledge that there is no true progress in human history, except perhaps in the slowly growing consciousness of the unifying forces within mankind. In spite of all the present threats to what is left of our civilization, I cannot give up hope that the two lines, that of man's share in history and that of God's part in it, far from being parallel or diverging, are coming closer and closer together. They may join one day.

[12] 'Awe is mankind's best part' (*Faust* II) – an inadequate translation, I fear.

Index

Index

Index

Index

Cilicia, 116

Cimon, 30

Clark, Sir G. N., 169

Claudius, 11

Cleanthes, 100 f.

Cleisthenes, 27

Cleitarchus, 91

Cleomenes III, 71 f., 85

Cleon, 21

Cleopatra, 11, 16, 131, 138

Columbus, 94

Constant, B., 25, 29, 31

Constantine, 14, 16, 125, 180

Constantinople, 2, 64

Copernicus, 95

Corinth, 53, 71 f., 74, 76

Cos, 70

Coulanges, Fustel de, 26

Crassus, 140

Craterus, 92

Crates of Thebes, 99

Crete, 4, 57 f.

Curtius, E., 26

Cybele, 105

Cynics, 99 f.

Cyprus, 76

Cyrene, 54, 70, 76

Dacia, 140

Dante, A., 127

Darius I, 153

Darwin, C., 158

Deiotarus, 131

Delacroix, E., 19

Delos, 74, 76

Delphi, 55, 71

Demaratus, 25

Demetrius of Phaleron, 57, 68, 90

Demetrius Poliorcetes, 139

democracy, 25, 27 f., 30 f., 47

Democritus, 100

Diadochi, 67 f.

Diaspora, 102 f., 175 f.

Dicaearchus, 94

Dickens, C., 166

Dike, 50 f.

Dio Cassius, 129, 134, 137

Diocletian, 14, 124, 173

Diodorus, 67

dioecetes, 80, 86

Diogenes (Cynic), 99

Diogenes Laertius, 93

Dion, 59

Dionysius (the elder), 55

Dionysius Thrax, 93

Dionysus, 48, 105

Dispersion, *see* Diaspora

Dorian, 4, 167

Dostoevsky, F., 179

Doura-Europus, 12 f., 79, 98

Droysen, J. G., 64 f.

Dubnow, S. M., 174

Duris, 92

Egypt, 2–4, 52, 56, 64 f., 67, 71 f.,
74, 76, 78–81, 83, 86 f., 90, 98,
106, 136, 175

Eleusis, 105

Elis, 71

Elton, G. R., 147

Ennius, 113

Epictetus, 102

Epicuraeans, 99–101

Epimetheus, 36 f.

Index

Epirus, 74
equality, 27
Eratosthenes, 94
Eros, 51
Etruscan, 6, 110, 139, 141
Euclid, 94
Eudoxus, 90
Euhemerus, 88, 93
Eumenes, 68
Eupolis, 61
Euripides, 46–50, 89, 91

federation, 77
Flaminius, T. Quintus, 73
Florianus, 124
France, A., 27, 167
freedom, 19–34, 82, 100
Froude, J. A., 154

Gades, 124
Galatians, 71, 74
Gallienus, 124
Gandhara, 98
Germans, 2, 17, 124
Gibbon, E., 13, 156
Glotz, G., 26
Goethe, J. W. von, 18, 35, 166, 182
Gracchi, 114, 120
Grote, G., 26
Grotius, H., 32

Hadrian, 172
Hammurabi, 3 f.
Hannibal, 72
Hanno, 94
Hardy, T., 171

Hegel, G. F. W., 165
hegemon, 77
Hephaestus, 35
Heraclitus, 42, 100 f., 168
Hermetica, 104
Hero of Alexandria, 95
Herod the Great, 102
Herodas, 91
Herodotus, 3, 21, 25, 27, 152
Hesiod, 5, 35–7, 41, 50
Hieron II, 70, 95
Hieronymus of Cardia, 67, 92
Hipparchus, 94 f.
Hippocrates, 161
Hippodamus, 12, 96
Hitler, A., 25
Hobbes, T., 32
Hölderlin, F., 26
Homer, 4, 6 f., 30, 36, 42, 44, 60, 93
Horace, 110, 121, 123
humanism, 181
Humboldt, W. von, 26, 31
Huns, 17
Huxley, J., 158

Ibsen, H., 47
Ikhnaton, 4
Ilium, 141
Illyria, 14, 72, 74
India, 2, 9 f., 66, 94, 99, 174
Indo-European, 1, 6
Inge, W. R. (Dean), 176
Ionian, 5
Iranians, 58, 71
Isis, 105
Islam, 6, 180
Isocrates, 55, 59, 61–3, 81, 88

Index

Index

Index